evolving through **ACTION**

Maximizing business returns by driving Action from the data warehouse

ROB ARMSTRONG AND DAN HIGGINS

Editing by Nancy Underwood
Cover design by Katherine McGee and Tacy Armstrong
Microsoft Clipart
ISBN – 0-9742728-0-9

We would like to express our thanks to all the people who helped make this possible. This includes the numerous customers and corporations from which most of these lessons were learned, sometimes the hard way. Of particular mention are those who allowed case studies to be included in this book.

In order to maintain the respect for our clients and customers, company names are only used with express permission or where the information was also made available in public forums such as conferences, articles or interviews.

We would also like to extend our thanks to all those who took time, and patience, to read the early drafts, offer opinions, and helped guide and shape our work.

Finally we would like to thank our families and friends for the support and encouragement that allowed us to toil along. In the end, it was with time away from them that we got the many hours to write the book.

Rob Armstrong – The Data Warehouse "Sherpa"

In the past, I have been introduced as the data warehouse sherpa. While this is some flattery, I like it because it describes what I strive to be in the warehouse arena.

A sherpa helps lead the climbers to the top of the mountain. They must know the conditions, the abilities of the climbers, the paths to take given the realities and challenges, the equipment necessary to have along, and many other factors. In short, they are the ones who have been there, know the way, and can help you achieve success. They are also the ones that are rarely mentioned in your success, but they take pride in knowing they helped you on your journey.

I think of this as I recall the term coined by Richard Winter, a data warehouse consultant best known for the Very Large Database report. The term is the "Everest Effect." Richard's point is that as data warehouse data volumes grow, small mistakes become fatal. You may be able to climb your neighborhood hill without proper shoes, a supply of food and water, and an oxygen bottle, but make those mistakes while climbing a real mountain and you will die. Successful data warehouse systems will grow well beyond anyone's thinking. If you are to be successful at the highest heights you need to have planned ahead a long time ago.

I want to use my background and experience in the data warehouse arena to be your sherpa to further success. I have helped design, implement, leverage, and justify data warehouse systems. I have led teams at production sites as well as led internal teams to plan out where the data warehouse arena is going, and more importantly, where it needs to be going.

But the lessons and examples in this book are not only about technology. They are also designed to help you exploit your data warehouse to a greater degree. What steps need to be taken next to further your capability and take you to even higher business return? What steps need to be avoided to keep from falling into a crevice, never to be heard from again? How can you motivate the business users to discover new insights? What is the role your IT department will have in this team? Are there other groups that need to be involved in this adventure?

The lessons are set out in an easy to read and understand manner. The stories and analogies are designed to communicate ideas and reinforce the value of the principles. In addition there are "Action Questions," questions or tasks that you should undertake to see how best to apply the lessons in your business at the end of each lesson.

Dan Higgins – The Data Warehouse "Golf Pro"

While Rob's analogy of a sherpa carries a tremendous sense of adventure – and data warehousing has a sense of adventure – I chose an analogy closer to home. For those of us who take the game of golf seriously, we also set our eyes on increasingly difficult goals. Not the highest mountain, but the lowest score.

As when exploiting technology to achieve a business goal, the eventual result in a game of golf is determined by a myriad of decisions and effective execution of those decisions. Fully realizing one's potential at the game of golf requires:

- Determining the best overall strategy for each hole on a given golf course.
- Determining the best tactic or approach for each shot, balancing risk and reward.
- Determining the most appropriate club with which to execute each shot.
- Effectively exploiting the chosen club to achieve the desired result on each shot.
- Recognizing that the result of each shot has a direct impact on the next.

Similarly, when considering the application of technology to achieve desired business results an organization must:

- Determine a strategy that will offer the greatest likelihood of success.
- Consider risk and reward for each step in the execution of the strategy. You want to minimize risk and maximize reward.
- Always select the best technology for a given task.
- Execute.

A serious golfer would not use a putter for a tee shot or a sand wedge to putt. Yet all too often we see organizations attempt to use the wrong tool for the wrong reason to solve business problems requiring data warehousing and decision support technology. Now, you might use a putter for every golf shot. But it will take you far longer and you certainly will not reach your goal of a low score!

Like Rob, I have been involved in numerous data warehousing projects, both as a customer and as a consultant. I have learned from both successes and mistakes, good shots and poor shots. And as with a good caddie or golf pro, I trust that my experience with this "course" will help you consistently improve your data warehousing skill, judgment and success.

Table of Contents

Preface – Driving Action

"The measure of success is not whether you have a tough problem to deal with, but whether it is the same problem you had last year."
John Foster Dulles, Secretary of State

When thinking about a title for our book, we tried many different options and phrasing. We kept coming back to the premise of action and evolution. Having said that, the title really refers to a variety of meanings.

The goal of any data warehouse environment is to drive business value. In order to do that, the environment must support the understanding, taking, and measuring of actions. Without action there is no return. Unfortunately, many people think that just by building the data warehouse the company will achieve the promises of the business plan.

It does not happen that way. The environment must be provided, but the evolution, from looking at reports, to making decisions, and finally taking action, must be nurtured at all times. So in one sense you must evolve the data warehouse to an action oriented state. However without measuring the effect of your actions, the actions themselves can be misdirected. Therefore you need to evolve not just to action but beyond it to measurement and understanding.

When you take actions, and measure their effects on your outcomes, you gain understanding about your business. This understanding of your actions, processes, and ultimately customers or suppliers, lead your business to evolve to a higher level of effectiveness. In short, you have evolved by taking actions.

Finally, the title refers specifically to the "E" of evolving. We see throughout our experiences that moving your data warehouse forward entails an ever increasing circle of "enable, encourage, embrace, and extend". These are the E's of data warehousing.

So having said all that, just what does the evolutionary path of the warehouse look like? We have all seen the picture depicting the evolution of man. It starts out on the far left hand side with an ape-like creature on all fours. As it progresses to the right the creature slowly becomes upright and more human looking. This graphic is applicable as we look at the evolution of the data warehouse environment as well.

Just as you cannot run before you walk, or walk before you crawl, your business cannot start off in the fully evolved endpoint. However, when looking at the business aspects of your environment, it is helpful to decide where you want to end up and then look backwards to where you need to begin.

As anyone can tell you, the "big bang" approach to a data warehouse is not feasible and the evolution is continuous. One does not start out with the "highly evolved environment". The evolution is never ending. If automation of your strategic and tactical practices is the goal, then you must first have the pieces in place to make this achievable.

In the case of the data warehouse, the business goal is to become as efficient and effective as possible when dealing with your customers, suppliers and internal processes. The zenith of such a state is the automation of routine business practices. You can actually see the business happen as it is happening, and then automatically apply business rules culled from strategic analysis to offer the right treatment at the right time. This is a concept we have called "*Automating your business*." Many of these concepts will be explored in more detail in the various sections of the book.

In order to determine how this evolves, it is best to look backwards with companies that have already reached an advanced state. Before knowing how to automatically respond to your business, you need to have the capability to see the business as it happens. It is no use knowing how to interact with your customers and processes if you cannot see them interacting with you. Every time delay from that point is only costing you money. This means that you need to have data on the transactions, and interactions, captured and available as soon as possible. This is a stage called "*Running your business as it happens*."

Stepping back in the evolutionary chain even further, we cross a chasm from the tactical to the strategic. This is the stage where you are finding the business rules and setting the practices for interactions. The real purpose of this stage is to predict how your business will respond when a set of events takes place. This phase is called "*Planning your business*."

In order for this stage to be most effective, you need to be able to see the whole business as a business but not necessarily as it happens. You cannot have a biased or incomplete view of trends and events. You must also have complete historic (and at times futuristic) relevant data. The quality of the data is an issue if not already tackled by this stage.

We continue the evolutionary trip back to a stage that most people are very familiar with and actually think of as the "data warehouse," though it is a far cry from a fully evolved environment (as we can now see!) This is the phase known as "*Understanding your business*."

This is the stage at which you get past a simple reporting business and into cross-functional analysis. You start understanding why things are happening and at many times can plan effective action to rectify problems or improve processes. Here you need to have more detailed data (in order to "drill down" into the why's) and you should be including a feedback loop from your actions into your processes.

The last phase we see, and the one where many people surveyed are at currently, is the stage of "*Seeing your business*." This means that your business users are able to get consistent reports on what happened, probably online and refreshed at a reasonable frequency.

Many people say they are at this initial stage but in reality they are back in the evolutionary equivalent of single cell creatures swimming aimlessly in sea of data. While the business users can get reports, the data is inconsistent; the information is rarely at the needed level of depth, or available in a timely enough manner as to truly effect any significant action. Yes, the major problems are highlighted and that sometimes gets the attention of management to bring pressure for fixes. These companies operate in what is known as crisis management. They can manage any event into a crisis and only when it gets to that point will they look at managing a solution!

So now that we have traveled back in the evolution of the data warehouse to gain our hindsight, let us put the evolution in order and see the business food chain (as those at the higher level will "eat" those at the lower end). The progression is as such:

1. Seeing your business	Consistent reports
2. Understanding your business	Cross functional, integrated detail data, analytical insight
3. Planning your business	Predictive and Causal relations are known and implemented
4. Running your business	Near time transactional data feeds, analysis possible as events occur
5. Automating your business	Business rules in place to initiate actions as a normal business practice

At each stage of the evolution you find that the business requires **more** users looking at **more** data, **more** frequently, with **more** cross functionality in order to ask for **more** analyses that requires **more** complexity. That is our "Mores' Law."

The evolution also shows an increase in productivity, effectiveness, and value at each step. To move from one stage to the next takes directed action and planning.

Where is your total business today? Where do you need to be, and when do you need to be there? Most importantly, what are you doing to get your company there? This is the crux of the evolution dilemma and the focus of this book.

When looking from the technology side it is helpful to work backwards from the future needs, but it is not practical to build the end-state as the first implementation. The architecture needs to be built upon itself as business evolution progresses. One of the realities in the IT arena is that our technology brethren are being asked to be more cost effective while at the same time being asked to deliver higher quality solutions at an ever increasing pace. In order to do this the IT groups want to have clearly defined requirements so projects can be scoped to ensure success. Unfortunately the business community cannot provide a rigorous set of detailed requirements because they live in an ever-present state of change.

That's why the data warehouse creates an environment that must always anticipate an ever-changing set of requirements. A paradoxical situation presents itself when trying to build such an environment.

If the data warehouse is designed and implemented on elements that are guaranteed to change you will create an environment that is unable to change. Conversely, if you design based on elements that are guaranteed not to change, you will encourage and increase the rate of change.

This is one of the critical messages. IT must first *enable an environment that will allow the business community to evolve.* There have been many books written on this topic and many of the messages are contained in Rob's first book, Secrets of the Best Data Warehouses in the World (Armstrong, Hanusa, and Coffing). The best practices of an enabled data warehouse architecture are also explored in the first chapter.

Clearly the IT group has certain responsibilities to deliver the environment, but the business users and executives have roles to play as well. This is not an environment of define and deliver. It is a constant path of *"enable, encourage, embrace, and extend."* It is this path we will explore in the following chapters.

To start with, let's first look at how the IT department can effectively, and efficiently, deploy a foundation to enable the business users to progress on the evolutionary path while at the same time avoid building the barriers that prevent the ensuing changes.

Enabling

The philosophy of the data warehouse is that it should support any analysis, against any data, for any business purpose, at any time.

As mentioned previously, many people undertake the development of the data warehouse as they would other technology projects. The project is turned over to the watchful eye of a technical lead who has experience in developing systems. Unfortunately the reason they are successful in systems development is the exact reason the data warehouse will present such a challenge.

While we were speaking to a room full of data technology professionals, one of the attendees mentioned that they understood data warehousing and they only wanted to know how our technology differed from other technology. At that point we asked a simple question, "What is the difference between a database and a data warehouse?" The room answered with silence. What is interesting is that this question has been asked before with responses all over the map. Some say that a database allows for any exploration, is highly flexible, and allows for normal relational models. They then say that data warehouses are static, read only, modeled for specific functions, highly controlled for performance, and the like.

The true answer to the question is that data warehousing is an approach to providing information that allows for asking any question against any data at any time, while a database is simply one of many tools that are employed in the building of a data warehouse. It is like asking what is the difference between a hammer and a house. One is used to build the other.

At the same time, another aspect of this philosophy is that while IT provides the analytical process, they should not own it. IT develops, maintains and manages the data, allowing the users the direct access via toolsets and applications. Business users are the "owners" of the data, IT professionals are the stewards of the environment.

By understanding your longer term strategy you will see the foundational requirements that will enable you to move forward quickly as opposed to constantly rebuilding the underlying foundation. While you cannot anticipate every, or any particular, analyses or questions, you can be guaranteed of the "Mores' law." You will be asked to provide *more* access to *more* data with *more* complexity and a *more* frequent update of *more* detail data. Plan for the environment to constantly change.

So when you are starting out with the data warehouse, look to see if you are really appreciating what the long term impact of your philosophy is going to be. Start building with the attitude "we don't want to inhibit that." As opposed to the classic IT response "we won't do that". Your data warehouse philosophy should enable evolution without barriers.

Action Questions:

- *What is your current vision and philosophy of the data warehouse?*
- *Are you anticipating, and therefore creating, the future or is the data warehouse there for reactive analysis?*
- *Is this vision shared across the company?*
- *Who truly owns the data warehouse program? How close are they to the business goals and challenges?*

Bring process to the data not data to the process

Distributed data forces centralized decision making. Centralized data enables distributed decision making.

So what exactly is the impact of this new philosophy? A major difference is that in order to allow all your users to ask any questions against any data, you need to bring that data together at some time. To achieve this, you can bring the data together initially, you can constantly forecast data requirements and move the necessary data to the necessary platform, or you can move the data at the time the query is asked. Typically, the movement of data either happens during the time of query or is defined for every new function. Data is moved and replicated in what is known as a "publish and subscribe" architecture.

The only philosophy that can support your ever increasing demands is to bring the data together once and then let any process ask any question of data whenever necessary. This way the data is always ready to be analyzed for all aspects of the business. The idea of anticipating all the data requirements in order to move the data around your environment is one that cannot be supported as the business accelerates the various processes.

This is an important point that is often left out of planning the early phases of the data warehouse. For any data element, there are many different processes and functions that need that data available. Usually they need to access the data in different ways with different frequencies. For example, one group may need information on a weekly basis but other groups in the business may need to see that same data on a daily or even more frequent basis. The best practice is to bring the data together at the lowest level of granularity, at the most frequent level possible and then let any process access the data as required.

One of the goals many companies have is to allow the customer "touch points" to make decisions and take actions at the time of interaction. In order to do this, the "touch point" (be it human or application) will need to have all relevant data available to make such decisions. The paradox in this environment is that by distributing data (i.e. take data to process) you actually force decisions and action to a central point, where the decisions are made as to what data each user can access. By centralizing the data (bringing process to data) you can effectively distribute the decision making process as all processes are able to get to any data necessary.

There is a final comment to note about this idea. As the business insight accelerates, the time lag between an event happening and the action needing to be taken shrinks. As this occurs the user community will ask for more capability to be delivered even quicker. Today, there are customers doing over 1 petabyte of data movement on a daily basis within centralized systems. This could not be accomplished if the data were not already centralized and integrated.

If your architecture is based on moving data to processes, every time you need to increase capability you will have a bigger problem to solve (as more data now needs to be consistent or moved). What is happening is that each subsequent improvement takes longer to deliver at the exact time that it needs to be delivered sooner! When you set up a "push" architecture this way, you are in for an ever diverging ability to meet new business requirements.

Action Questions:

- *What are your guidelines on replicating data?*
- *In how many places do you keep the same information?*
- *When you need to find data elements, do your users need to first find out where the information is before they understand how they can work with it?*
- *If your data volume, data elements, or data usage suddenly doubled, what impact would that have on your total environment?*
- *Are you trying to distribute decision-making? How does your current environment enable that capability?*

There should be no centricity to a data model

If design is based on elements that are guaranteed to change, you will create an environment that is unable to change.

As the drive to bring more and more customer focused processes into the data warehouse arena continues, one of the common barriers companies face is moving from a product centric model to a customer centric one. In the rush to provide users these urgent capabilities, the implementers cannot see that they are about to make the same mistake that was made the first time: namely, they give centricity to the data model.

Centricity is a functional concept. Your business will require many different functions to process and analyze data in many different ways. The data warehouse is not only for the customer relationship applications; it must also support inventory, segmentation, order processing, resource allocations and a whole host of other functions. And in the end, aren't all of these processes in support of serving the customer better and running a more effective business?

The ideal data warehouse model has no centricity at the base level. One needs to keep the model neutral and allow all functions to see the business as they need to when situations arise. You can think of this as either being omni-centric or anti-centric. This point is heresy to many in the business, as it raises the challenge for the database and data modeler to a new level. Despite this obvious break with popular opinion, this thought will stand the test of time and be seen as an obvious requirement for future successes.

Remember, no one knows what the next big revolution in data warehousing and business is going to bring. If you start to focus in on customers at the expense of all else then you will eventually end up with a system that will not support the inclusion of non-customer specific processes. You will be creating your model on a dimension that is sure to change in time.

The bottom line is that data has no centricity. It is simply data. On the other hand, centricity is a concept borne of usage and therefore subject to change. Look to the past to see that this is correct. We used to think a product centric model would give the most insight, but these models are failing. Centricity should be created in your logical views not your physical model. This way you are welcoming change as opposed to fearing it.

Action Questions:

- *How was your model initially created?*
- *What assumptions were made about its evolution?*
- *Are the logical and physical models significantly different? If so, why is that?*
- *When change occurs in your process, how readily can you accommodate that change in your warehouse?*

Performance should be a business metric

There is no point in carrying the ball if you don't know where the goal is.

One of the most telling aspects of the intent of the data warehouse is understanding how success is being measured. We are always amazed when people start asking how many queries can be accommodated by a system. They also put forth acceptance criteria such as query run times, queries per second and the like. The data warehouse is not a traditional operational system. It is an environment for new insight and exploration. Acceptance criteria need to consider issues such as "what new queries will I be able to ask," "how deep can I drive my analysis," "how wide across my organization can I see my processes," or "how many new actions were created."

Clearly there is a need to understand the capacity of a system and understand how many concurrent users can be accessing the system, but those are secondary metrics. It does not help that 100 people can run queries simultaneously if they can only ask questions that return very little insight. To get the usual metrics, systems are too often compromised by heavy indexing, functionalization of the model, or limiting usage to aggregated answer sets. All of this goes contrary to the real purpose and philosophy of building the data warehouse.

To determine the success of the data warehouse one must have measurable return on investment metrics in place at the start of the program, not years later. A colleague once stated that if you can not measure the value of the warehouse with the warehouse then you got it wrong.

This all comes back to the idea that you must build in the Return On Investment (ROI) measurement and metrics up front when designing your data warehouse. What was the business case for the system or application? How was that represented in the budget? Many companies are now starting to either increase revenue targets or place a line item expense in for the warehouse itself. If this system is really critical to the business then the users and business management will need to commit dollars to the process and success should be measured by the return on those investments, not by the return time of the queries.

Action Questions:

- *What metrics do you use to judge the value of the warehouse?*
- *What form of measurement do you have against the planned ROI?*
- *Who is responsible for tracking this information?*
- *Do new applications require a business case with ROI measurements before funding? Are those measurements engrained into the warehouse metrics?*

Data Quality – valid, accurate, and complete

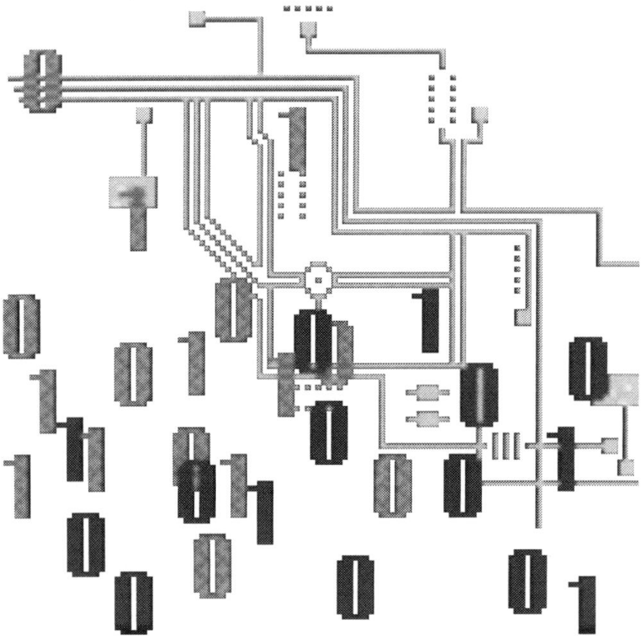

They have one language and this is only the beginning of what they will do and nothing they propose to do will now be impossible for them
Genesis 11:6 (Tower of Babel)

The importance of data quality cannot be overstated. The data in your warehouse is what is used to create, drive, and refine your business strategies. As the environment evolves and real time actions are incorporated, the data is affecting your direct interactions with your process. If the data quality is suspect or knowingly bad, then users will lose confidence and decisions will lead to undesired outcomes.

Data quality has several aspects and each can stand on its own. The most critical are the completeness and accuracy of the data. Easier issues to address are the precision and the validity of the data. Let's walk through an example and then look at possible alternatives for cleansing the data.

Assume you have data regarding your customers in the data warehouse. You may have name, address, income, and family size. The easiest aspect of quality to check is validity. Typically this is format or range checking. Is the address numeric? Does the zip code match for city-state pairing? Is the family size within a reasonable range, say less than 15? Often times the data fields become corrupt as people start using enterprise wide fields for local purposes. Generally it is the responsibility of the front end application to perform these checks.

Once you have valid data you look at accuracy. This is a little tougher as it typically requires contact with the true owner of the data (such as the customers themselves) and that may not be feasible for all your data elements. You can also look at several data elements in concert to highlight possible inconsistencies. For example, does the income correspond with the demographic for the area? Do the buying patterns seem to bear out the family size (there are 4 Christmas club accounts but the customer has 6 children)? While you cannot always correct the data through this process you can highlight areas that need to be followed up, or find possible opportunities in the data (for example, market the customer for more Christmas club accounts).

A comment about getting verification of data from the customers. In order for people to give you personal details they need to have an incentive to do so. What are they getting in terms of payback? If they think they will be tele-marketed, junk mail-ed, or annoyed then there will be a huge reluctance to providing details. On the other hand, if your customers perceive they will get value by better targeted offers, better discounts, or more selection of services then they will be more open to sharing. Another aspect of this is you need to collect data in a way that is relevant to the customer. Are you collecting the phone number during a cash sale? Many people do not see the correlation between the event and the request and are therefore hesitant to provide information.

The next aspect, completeness, is another one where you may need to draw inference from other data. You will also need to ensure a feedback loop from actions to response. What data is missing to make better decisions? Do I need the age of the household members? Do I need to know their genders? Can I get that from the clothing purchases I track? The real answer is that your data will rarely ever be complete as you can constantly add more knowledge to your decision. The question is what missing data would be the most valuable and the most reasonable to obtain. Many companies often overlook this as they do not go back to study their processes to see what was missing in the analysis.

The good news for the IT community is that most of the responsibility for data quality falls on the user community. They need to define what is valid. Business rules must be created to determine accuracy and the level of completeness necessary to support the business process. It is also up to the user community to determine the corrections when data quality is suspect. The user community should "own" the definition of the data. The hard part for the IT community is that once these rules and definitions are established, it is up to IT to ensure adherence to them. This is an area in which cooperation and communication is of utmost importance.

Action Questions:

- *What is your current process for judging, and fixing, data quality issues?*
- *How much of the data quality is pushed back to the originating systems?*
- *Do your core data elements have business owners identified?*
- *Are you giving your customers an incentive for you to have valid and complete information?*

You only see a fraction of what you need

It's not so much what folks don't know that causes problems, it's what they do know that ain't so.

– Artemus Ward

Often times in discussions with companies you will hear a comment to the effect of "We can provide about 80% of what the users need from the current systems, so why change?" That would be a valid argument if only it were true. Unfortunately it is far from the truth and the attitude actually inhibits you from enabling any type of evolution.

Let's start by looking at the comment. "We can provide 80% of what the users need." That implies that you know what 100%. Often companies do not know what users need to do in the next few months, let alone the coming years. Given that, how can the statement be made that 80% of the necessary capability is currently available? What is really being said is that 80% of what is being asked for can be provided.

The second problem with the statement is that it implies that even though you know you need that last 20% more information, it cannot be delivered in a cost effective manner. Now comes the question of whether or not you are willing to let technology barriers stop your business. You should at least explore the options to see if you truly cannot provide the next level of analysis.

An offshoot of this attitude is that the data is typically being pre-packaged and in most cases summarized in order to be cost effective. Summaries will not give an accurate picture of the business as they represent situations that do not exist. For example, we have yet to see a household with 2.3 children. Information like this actually has negative value as it leads to mis-directed actions.

The real issue for the "80%ers" is they are not providing 80% of what they need or anything close to that number. What they are providing is 80% of the known requests. Here is an analogy. When you were a child, your world was your back yard. As you approached adulthood, you went to school, learned to drive and gained more freedom. As this growth occurred you realized there was so much more to your world. Your backyard was now only a small portion of what was really important. Today, you can get in a plane and realize your backyard is not even 1% of the possibilities. The more you know, the more you realize you don't know.

This means that as your environment evolves, it will spawn a greater need to further evolve, and at a greater pace. One customer calls their data warehouse the "passport system." This is a great name as it conveys the ability to explore, see new areas, and gain new knowledge about their business.

So ask yourself, how much of what you could do, can you do? Then check to make sure your passport has not expired so you can see your world.

Action Questions:

- *What is the process for users discovering new opportunity for analysis?*
- *What are your barriers and thresholds to new lines of inquiry?*
- *How capable is the environment supporting the "unknown"?*
- *Do you heas statements like "we don't think we'll ever ask that question" or "We don't see the users asking for that data?"*
- *Have your users stopped asking for new capability? A silent user community is not necessarily a happy one.*

Spirals Within Spirals

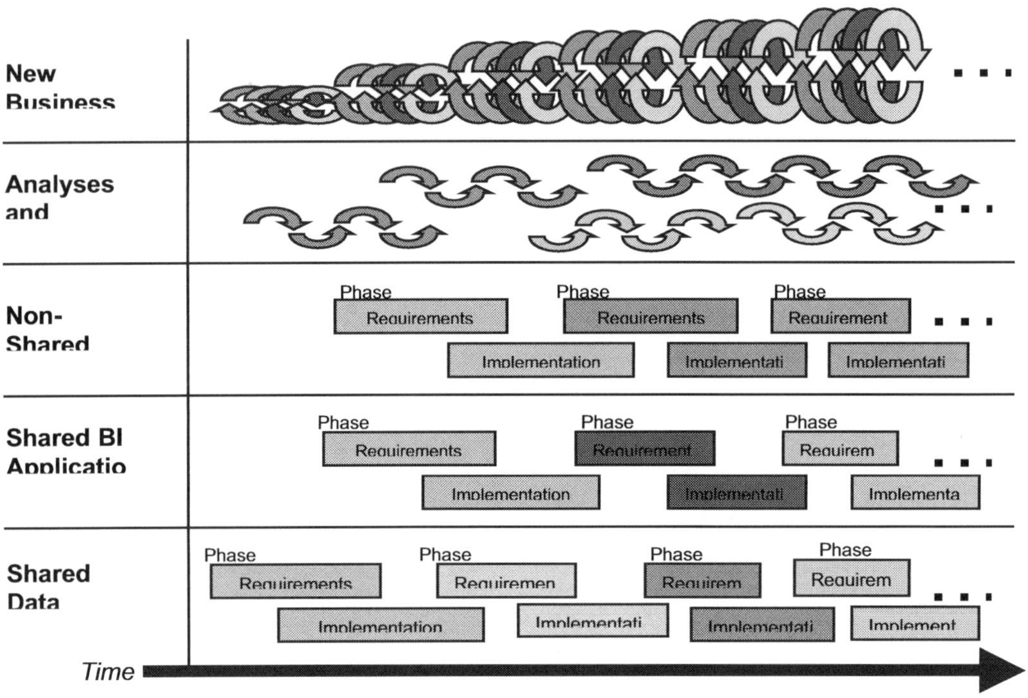

Alpha and Omega, the end is the beginning, the last step is the first.

Classic IT processes are not effective when it comes to data warehousing and decision support. How many times when the business goes to IT with a request have you heard (or said), "it will take 3 months and $100,000." How often does this occur because the IT processes and bureaucracy – very important for the management and control of some IT assets – have become an impediment to effective decision support?

The varying and constantly changing decision support needs of the business not only require an agile and adaptive technology infrastructure, but also flexible and accommodating IT processes. Operational applications based on well understood business processes and requirements are usually developed using a "waterfall" engineering approach. The waterfall approach involves an end-to-end sequence of sometimes lengthy phases including requirements, design, code, test and deployment. But in decision support, IT not only needs to provide the business with applications, but also an environment that supports short term studies and analyses and ad hoc, "use once, throw away" business questions.

The "spiral" approach to software engineering became well known in the 1980's as a more effective means of evolving applications and information systems over time while delivering business value along the way. With the spiral model the necessary elements of requirements, design, code, test and delivery are compressed into short time frames. These phases are overlapped and the complete sequence is iterated in a cyclical fashion. Each cycle delivers additional capability – thus the term "spiral."

In data warehousing and decision support, we see the need for spirals, fast spirals and very fast spirals. Some data warehousing work requires more planning and coordination than other. This occurs with "Extract, Transform, and Load (ETL)" work, especially early in the life of a data warehouse, and with shared assets – both data and applications. But as more data is added to the data warehouse, there should be increasing opportunity for rapid applications, short term studies, data analysis and single-use ad hoc business questions.

Thus, the healthy decision support system (DSS) environment will have a variety of IT processes, spirals within spirals, to balance the need for managing shared assets while enabling the responsiveness and flexibility needed for decision support.

Action Questions:

- *What processes do you have in place to accommodate unforeseen business questions that need answers today?*
- *Do you have lightweight procedures for business that need to perform short-duration analyses and studies on the data warehouse?*
- *How do you manage change in the shared data structures while allowing access to a variety of applications and business users?*
- *Do you have any implementation projects taking longer than 90 - 120 days? (You shouldn't).*

Are you solving non-problems of the past or understanding the challenges of the future?

Build for the future, it will be here when you are done.

The last lesson of the enabling section asks you to question what you are trying to enable. As was pointed out before, most companies look at the needs of today and try to meet them with tomorrow's implementations. Understand that any implementation will be delivered at a future date, by definition, and therefore the changing needs must be taken into account.

You see this in many different industries. For example, retailers that do not "get it" will worry about the out of stock reports. They constantly try to manage the symptom (no stock) rather than the disease (bad inventory management). If they would look past the situation to understand the real problems then they could proceed to implement solutions that truly allow investigation and insight into the inventory management area. Once that is understood, many other aspects of the company could be addressed.

This was illustrated in great form at one retailer. The users said they wanted to understand inventory positions, as they did not have the ability to look at the detailed data. After several months of work, the IT group delivered a series of reports that gave details on what the user asked for. Unfortunately, in the words of one user, "It took 6 weeks to see yesterday's data." This means that any decision and action that would be made was worthless. The real requirement is the ability to see the inventory position, at a detailed level, in a timely manner to effect change.

This is one of the underpinnings of a successful data warehouse implementation. The IT group must understand that they are providing a solution that is to address the challenges of the future and as such, cannot demand detailed requirements from the users. The IT group must provide all the enabling foundations and then allow user groups to drive the performance and flexibility by exploiting those foundations.

Why is this so important to understand? Because when the technology groups pick the tools which will enable true data warehousing, the decision criteria usually looks at what is happening in the business today. The evaluations are based on "speeds and feeds". Change your evaluations to focus on providing a future for the business as opposed to cementing the present processes in place.

Action Questions:

- *How were your tools chosen?*
- *Do they inhibit or enable the users to see the business change as the business changes?*
- *Do your IT standards reflect the needs of a changing business environment?*

The best way to solve any problem is to remove its cause.
- Martin Luther King, Jr.

One of the ways we can validate the recommendations and lessons in this book is to see how they work in reality. To that end, we have included real world examples at the end of each of the major sections. The enabling case study is from the work done at Travelocity, an Internet travel planning company.

The company was about to experience an explosive growth rate. The competition for online services was increasing and the company was demanding more returns from their efforts. The existing data warehouse system had been built from a functional perspective to provide reports to decision makers and business users. In order to compete in the coming months and years, it was apparent that they were going to have to become closer to the customer and understand individuals better. Unfortunately the existing solutions did not allow for that level of detailed analysis and it was questionable as to whether or not the environment would be able to handle the tremendous data increase that was necessary for the business community.

This company did something that few companies had done in the past. They decided to put everything on the table for evaluation. The tools and processes were examined to see if they moved the company to where they needed to be. If they weren't, they were open for replacement. While this could be an expensive undertaking, and many shy away from this path, it is much cheaper and less risky than trying to make unsuitable products and processes do the work.

The company changed many aspects of their existing data warehouse technology. They brought in new tools, developed cohesive models, and incorporated new front end tools. The end result has been astounding. Where there used to be a handful of IT programmers who had access to the data, now there are over 50 business users who have direct connection to the information they need to make decisions. Processes have been automated and streamlined to where rather than taking days to see what is happening, they can know in hours if problems, or opportunities, exist and can take decisive action quickly.

This is not to say that all their problems are solved and Travelocity can now sit back on past success. Now that they have taken the time and efforts to create the enabled environment, it is time to face new challenges. The next phase is the harder part and is explored in the following sections; the encouragement of new usage and directing actions from the data warehouse.

Encouraging

I have yet to find the man, however exalted his station, who did not do better work and put forth greater effort under a spirit of approval than under a spirit of criticism.
- Charles Schwab

It is often bewildering how much time and effort companies will invest in the data warehouse decision making process while letting the resulting implementation be a matter of chance. For some reason, many companies forget that executive commitment, and involvement, is not only necessary but often critical.

Obviously there was a business case to the data warehouse and therefore some expectations have been set as to what the users are going to do with the system. In order to ensure the quick adoption of the new solution, the executive group needs to also use and recognize the value of the system.

Examples of this would be the reporting and celebration of success metrics, meetings where information and insight from the system is shared with others, providing both business usage and technical content education, and holding people accountable for what was promised in the business plan. Without actions such as these, the new system will not have the push some users need in order to adopt the new ways.

Part of this is also change in culture. The data warehouse should be giving you insight into your policies and processes. As you gain more insight, these policies will most likely change. When politics or the "that is not how we used to do it" culture raises its ugly head, it typically requires a strong executive show of support to resolve those challenges.

Data warehousing is not like the typical operational system. In the world of operations, the benefits are obvious, either the promised process works or it doesn't. Either the bills get generated and mailed or they don't. Once it works there is little change to the environment.

In the warehouse arena the benefit, and success, is a little harder to realize. Are actions being taken? Are the decisions "better" than before? Is the warehouse responsible for the success of the last marketing program or is it the user who initiates action? All of these questions will arise and they cause battles as to the value, and success of the warehouse implementation.

Once again it comes down to leadership and vision. You should not have to find those qualities at the bottom of the corporate hierarchy. Lead by example, show your users and IT personnel that the company is solidly behind the new capability and it will quickly become adopted.

Encouraging Data Warehousing ROI

Not everything that can be counted counts,
Not everything that counts can be counted.
- Albert Einstein

If you are a senior executive or CEO of a company, what magnitude of return are you realizing from your data warehousing and decision support efforts? Do you or anyone on your staff track the ROI? Is this left with your IT group? Is it assigned to the business units responsible for using the systems to affect a return? Both? A data warehousing and decision support environment done correctly will be a significant investment in people and technology. There are tremendous opportunities for a return on that investment, but only if IT and the business units are strongly encouraged to work together to realize that ROI.

Planning, measuring and tracking ROI is not an exact science. But it does not need to be an exact science. Yes, there are tools and financial models that will help, but they are only as good as the input data and they will not cover every scenario. It is not necessary to measure and track ROI to two decimal places in order to understand the benefits of the investment. However it is important to understand the magnitude and the variety of benefits possible from the data warehouse.

First, you want to capture the benefits of a data warehouse because it will keep your organization focused on what really matters – business impact. Second, you want to capture the benefits so that you avoid the endless, counter-productive churning on technology decisions. Everyone tracks the costs (although in most cases, not all the costs). If you don't track the benefits, you are in danger of short-changing one of your most significant business improvement tools.

In our section on "Embracing Data Warehousing ROI" we will touch on types of "return" from your data warehousing investment and the fact that this return has more to do with business decision making and business execution than with the technology or IT savings. But typical IT budgets are only 2-4% of revenue and even cutting IT budgets in half would have minimal impact on the overall success of the organization when compared with the financial benefits from business improvements.

IT and business units look at ROI from opposite sides of the same coin. IT tends to be focused on cost and cost savings. Too few IT executives fully appreciate the potential for business improvement. On the other side of the coin, most business unit executives are focused on their area of responsibility and sometimes miss the opportunities that exist with the sharing of data. And they rarely appreciate the challenges faced by IT.

For this reason we believe that data warehousing and decision support ROI should be planned, measured and tracked by a steering committee involving both IT and the business. The chairperson for this committee should be someone from the business or someone reporting directly to the CEO with cross-functional oversight. This incorporates all perspectives while emphasizing the ultimate reason for the investment – business insight and improvement.

Action Questions:

- *Are you capturing the return from your data warehousing investments or only the costs?*
- *Are you capturing all of the people and process costs or simply the technology investments?*
- *Do you have a cross functional team that establishes the priorities, plans the investments and measures and reports the returns from your data warehouse?*

Decisions are easier when values are known.

While growing up, kids are always asked what they want to be. Typically the answers are astronauts, cowboys, firemen, pilots, ballerinas, and zookeepers. No one ever says they want to be a data warehouse sherpa or golf pro! The answers are based on the desire to have a seemingly exciting career.

When in college, students are again asked what do they want to do. At this point, the answers get a bit more realistic, but they tend to be centered around money. Students want to be doctors, lawyers, CEOs, or that ever-elusive "management." No one wants to be the worker bee.

As you progress in your career, you are asked, "Where do you want to go?" and, "What is your five year plan?" The answers to these questions start getting more varied as you understand what is really important in your life. If you like working with people, you move to an external or public facing job. If you want more control, you work towards an executive position. If you want more time with your family, you get a job where you have flexible hours or no travel.

The data warehouse environment is very similar. Consultants constantly want to know what you are trying to do with the environment and where you expect the data warehouse to take you. The answers to these types of questions are best known when you understand your values and guiding principles.

One of the ways that executives can encourage the data warehouse environment is by establishing, and supporting, key guiding principles. What are the five to ten "golden rules" which will guide your decision making process? It is important to not have too many as then you tend to have "principles" that contradict each other. Think of the Tax code versus the Ten Commandments. There is not a lot of cheating room with the commandments yet people cheat on taxes everyday, despite the thousands of pages of "rules".

The following are suggestions of the type of "principle statements" that can be used. Obviously each company is different and has different objectives. Consider these an example or something to start from and adapt them to your particular situation.

1) *The users will be able to access the data without delay caused by any other processes*. Very simply, the users should be able to ask any question against any data in the warehouse at any time. The users should also be able to ask queries and analysis that may take hours of processing. Loads, archives, and data management processes should not take any data element "off-line." The goal is for total, 24-7 data accessibility, not just system availability.

2) *The data model will reflect the business not the functions of the day*. This is a big one. The main data model for the warehouse needs to be neutral to the

functions being asked for, so that any question can be asked. Once that is ensured, views can be implemented to logically functionalize data subject areas. Another aspect of this philosophy is that data should be held at the lowest atomic level possible.

3) *There will be no artificial barriers to loading the data*, and when necessary, data can be loaded into the environment in "real time." Real time is relative to the need of the users and processes. For some data elements, it is OK to have daily updates while other elements need to be updated or inserted within minutes of the event occurring. This allows your users to see the business change as it is changing. The basic ramification is that the traditional batch process mentality needs to be re-addressed.

4) *The data warehouse will reflect the data from the operational system*. Where data discrepancies are identified, the operational system will be corrected as opposed to changing the data in the warehouse exclusively. In the end, you want to see all the stages and data points as opposed to just the "end state" of the data. With this information, the data warehouse will be able to help identify total process inefficiencies, direct strategies, and enhance business decisions.

This cannot be done effectively when the data in the data warehouse does not accurately reflect the data in the operational systems. Clearly there will be some data transformation but the context of the data should not be restructured. As data quality issues are identified, the data will need to be corrected via the operational systems and the data re-loaded (or the changes inserted) into the warehouse under the normal data flows.

5) *Data replications shall be held to a minimum*. It is the responsibility of the IT department to decide on data propagation and replication as this affects the whole architecture. This is done to provide the most timely, most consistent view of the business possible.

In functionally separate systems, application developers and business analysts like to jump quickly to adding indexes, changing data models, and creating summaries. In an enterprise data warehouse all of these actions can have significant impact to other business areas. It is incumbent on the IT group to become the stewards of the data and ensure an enterprise wide data foundation. IT should lead the decisions to optimize data structures and manage data replication.

6) *New subject areas will need to be justified with a business case*. This is to include an understanding of how to measure the ROI of the subject area.

While the steering committee and the program board need to have an identified path to adding new data elements, there will always be groups wanting their data on the data warehouse earlier than planned. The best way to manage this is to use business cases and ROI to help prioritize requests. This will help the decision-makers to effectively lead the warehouse evolution. It will also help in understanding what will be affected in the event timelines are adjusted for a variety of reasons.

Also by using this process the idea of prototypes can be used to quickly determine the extent of the ROI expectations. Business cases can quickly be validated and critical project criteria can be ascertained. The prototypes can also be useful in understanding the data elements necessary for new business opportunities.

7) *The key goal for the warehouse is ability to influence and enhance action-taking processes*. The goal is for actionable information as opposed to simple report functionality. The real purpose of the data warehouse is to move business decisions forward and improve the way people are looking at the business. There needs to be a move from looking "at data" to looking "for opportunities." This guideline is to help instill a culture into the business community and help prioritize requirements that go beyond "just providing reports."

As you read though the following lessons, the ideas behind the above principles are looked at in a variety of ways. This can help you gain a better understanding of the business impact from failure to follow your principles.

Action Questions:

- *Take a look around your organizations. Do you have a steering committee to lead the data warehouse evolution?*
- *Do you have guiding principles, and if so, how many are there (too many is as bad as not enough!)?*
- *Are they adhered to or referenced in decision making?*

Response time starts way before the enter key is pressed

It is the time from event to action that counts!

One of the common challenges to overcome in moving the data warehouse forward is the perception of response time. This is due to many systems being built as basic report generation environments. In the effort to get the warehouse delivered and accepted, the users were promised faster and better access to data. Unfortunately the benchmark the data warehouse is measured against is the current operational or pushed report systems. This means that users often expect a "sub-second" or few-second response time for all queries. In the end, "better" gets sacrificed for "faster."

One of the goals of executive encouragement is to get users away from a seconds per query mentality into a value per analysis mode. A large part of this process is to understand what real response time means in this new environment. As mentioned, most people will measure the time between hitting the enter key (or rather, clicking the OK button) and when the screen gets painted as response time. In the data warehouse world that is a largely useless measure.

In data warehousing the response time needs to be measured from the time a user has a thought until the time they have enough information in order to initiate action. Of course this can vary greatly. A report may show that revenue is down in the Northeast, so now the user has an avenue to explore, but no actions to take. How soon after this will the user be able to explain the revenue dip? How long until there is action to correct the situation?

In the un-enabled environment, the response time may be weeks as the user must get IT involved. IT will need to analyze requirements, create extracts and new aggregations and post the data during normal batch processing. The problem is exacerbated by the fact that the user will not only have to ask one extra question but possibly 3 to 5 new questions, each one getting more detailed along the way. In one company, the comment was made that it takes at least 3 weeks and $100,000 (this is what we refer to as the "pain threshold") to ask for any new aggregation of data. By the time those users get answers, they are likely to be no longer actionable or valuable.

A few more words about the concept of a "pain threshold." When it takes days and thousands of dollars to get new analysis, users are discouraged from trying new things. If you can lower the threshold to minutes or hours and the cost to tens or hundreds of dollars, you will motivate people to explore. If it only takes 10 minutes to set up and run a new line of inquiry, then, as a user, I can run almost 50 in one day! In that situation you do not care if 45 of them proved to be dead ends, you still get 5 new insights. In the old model, these 50 queries would have taken months to accomplish. Lower the price and pain of exploration and people will naturally explore.

Once the environment has been enabled, executives can work to change the mind set from one of getting reports to one of taking action. The key is that the users must be encouraged to try new analysis and to start looking for things in the processes that need to be changed. Unfortunately many people do not feel they have any ability to drive change, so they do not bother to look for the opportunity in the first place.

After that is accomplished, there is a further refinement of response time. The next level of response time is to understand the duration from the time an event occurs to the time you measure the value of the action. This means you must not only include the lag time between the event happening and the users seeing the event in reports or analysis, but also the time it takes for action to be initiated, responded to, and measured. Of course this response time will also vary greatly. However, it starts to focus your attention and processes onto what the customers themselves are experiencing. To the customers, this is response time. They do not care how your internal processes work, they only know it takes weeks to months before attractive offers are made available to them, or more importantly, corrective action is taken on their problems.

Action Questions:

- *How are you measuring the effectiveness of your warehouse?*
- *What is required for a user to explore a new avenue of analysis?*
- *Is the "pain threshold" to analysis low enough to encourage new exploration?*
- *How were performance requirements determined by the users? How were they accepted by IT?*

What gets measured gets done, and what gets done should be celebrated

A little praise goes a long way.
- Ralph Waldo Emerson

Why do people set milestones for projects? When this thought-provoking question is asked, most typical answers will be about having to show results to executives, needing to focus people on the challenge, and the like. While all those are very valid and correct answers, there is a better one.

We measure to have reason to celebrate. We need to set goals so that we can achieve them, celebrate our success and renew our efforts to the next milestone. This is the way you encourage people to try again and harder. It builds momentum and encourages innovation.

What is often missing in the evolution of the warehouse is the celebration part. Milestones are set from a technical level and there is business justification of the project but rarely do people communicate, and more importantly, celebrate that success. This means that users, who leverage the warehouse well, do not see the rewards of changing their processes, and those not using the warehouse do not see any motivation to change. It also means that typically IT is unaware of the tremendous value they are enabling and instead know only of the complaints and pressures to "do more with less."

The executives must understand that what a solid data warehouse can accomplish is significant change in the organization, internal practices, and cross-functional processes. The user community must see that the data warehouse is viewed as a strategic and powerful tool. All of this does not happen by accident, nor does it continue without constant vigilance. As with all things, the data warehouse will generate momentum but it never hurts to give it a "push" every once in a while. Without re-investing in the energy around the data warehouse it will lose momentum and stop.

People naturally want to be recognized for achievement. The outcome of the celebration of success is continued success. Once the users see that the company is behind the data warehouse efforts and values the results, the users become motivated to drive ahead even more. The business feels the momentum of new development and insight and the users get involved during the up front processes. This again increases the speed of development as well as sets realistic expectations.

But the celebration should not only be within the user community, it must also be in the IT groups as well. For many, the role of IT is one of resolving problems. As such, the job is one where all you hear all day is problems! In our company, we have customers visit our development facilities to speak to the designer and developers of our products. Often times the technical people express how glad they are to know their hard work and efforts are having a positive impact for our customers. Remember the success of business could not happen if the ability was never enabled!

The last part of this celebration and success is that it ingrains the idea that measurement and feedback are critical to the total process. If you are not measuring your success, how do you know you are being successful?

Action Questions:

- *When was the last time you communicated, and celebrated, a success from the data warehouse?*
- *Are your milestones business or technically oriented?*
- *How many of your users could name the major business metrics being driven from the data warehouse?*
- *How is your success communicated?*

Re-align compensation for consistent results

Actions follow conviction, not knowledge.
- Pierre LeComte

Of all the challenges you have in the data warehouse arena, the most difficult are the non-technical ones. These are the barriers around politics, culture, process, and ownership. Whenever we talk with executives, there will be at least one question on how to attack these problems. The good news is that you are not alone in facing these problems; the bad news is that the creation of the data warehouse will only highlight these challenges.

In almost every business decision, people will factor in many aspects before making decisions and taking action. In the typical environment of operational systems these factors are internal to a small fraction of the organization. In the data warehouse there is a different paradigm. The inherent value is not well known, it is not seen as a mission critical environment, and resources will be needed that take away from the traditional role of IT processes. Right off the bat, the challenges in bringing a data warehouse into existence and to continue leveraging the environment, are facing an uphill battle.

That however is not the real issue. The largest issue that will be raised by the data warehouse is that of data definitions and data consistency. As the data warehouse will be aimed at bringing the data of the business together, it is critical that the data be consistent and the business agree on what the data means. Who owns the data? Who is responsible for cleansing the data? What are the auditing rules to ensure the operational and informational systems are equivalent? All these questions arise and resources, effort, and time are all dependant on the answers. Groups that are already under strain to produce results will now be required to take on additional workloads.

Another reason for the highlighting of the political problems is that as data is called into question, existing practices and rules will also be questioned. It is human nature to want to be perceived as correct and any doubt on our decisions or practices makes us defensive. This is where the executive encouragement must be handled with the utmost care. This is not a problem of someone being right or wrong, it is a situation whereby the individual actions hamper the total process in a cross functional world. Often metrics and incentives will need to be rethought to encourage consistent behavior.

For example, if IT is motivated to keep costs low and business is motivated to increasing revenue, these may be at cross purposes. At one company, the IT manager was paid hundreds of thousands of dollars in bonuses over his career for not spending money on technology to move the business forward. Once the inconsistency was unearthed, it was a simple matter to re-align the processes, and politics, so IT and business had a common goal of increase market share and competitive advantage.

Action Questions:

- *Follow the money. How are your compensation metrics inter-linked across various functions?*
- *Are you encouraging behavior that is ultimately counter productive to your business?*
- *Do you have business units that won't "share," and if so, how do you make sure they have a vested interest in a total data warehouse success.*

The Encouraging Case study

I like things to happen; and if they don't happen, I like to make them happen.
- Winston Churchhill

There are many ways for executives to encourage usage in the data warehouse. These range from simple but direct communication of the change to the business, to reminding people at every opportunity of the role the data warehouse is playing in creating new insight. The critical element is that the business community must be given a clear message that executives fully support the data warehouse strategy and fully expect the full leverage of the environment to continually improve the business metrics.

For this section, we have selected two scenarios. The first is where the company encouraged this usage and environment by putting its money where its mouth was, literally. The company would collect user stories on the type of analysis that was done, the type of actions taken because of that analysis, and then the payback driven from those actions. For each story that showed a reasonable return, the user would get $50. The intent here was to foster some good-natured competition between the users, and motivate them to drive deeper analysis and communicate their success to others. The general feeling among executives was even if they paid out $5,000 or $10,000 each quarter, it was worth it as then they were collecting 100 to 200 success stories from the business community.

In an added twist to this, each quarter there was a newsletter that highlighted 4 of the success stories (one for each main business metric being tracked) and the contributing person was again paid money for this recognition. Users were competing to see who could provide the greatest example of payback to be in the quarterly newsletter.

The second case study is Harrah's Entertainment, a company that again had tremendous backing and support from the executive community. This was shown in the way decisions were made and funding for projects was approved. When one business unit wanted to build a new property, the request and budgets were taken to the executive officers. They questioned the business unit on the assumptions and wanted to know how the information in their data warehouse supported the building decision. The business unit went back and after a thorough analysis, discovered that the proposed new building was actually too small for the expected demand. As such, plans went forward on a larger investment. This showed the executives were willing to provide funding, and even expand funding, on analysis that was complete and compelling.

Harrah's also regularly highlights the achievements of the IT community and the data warehouse. This has been documented in the Wall Street Journal and their annual report heralds the success and contribution of the system to the bottom line. In such an atmosphere, there are few users who are willing to make decisions without first supporting their actions with facts from the enterprise data warehouse.

Embracing

Going to church doesn't make you religious, just as going to the garage does not make you a mechanic.

Two of the more frequent questions we get from companies using a data warehouse are: "How can I justify this to my executives?" and "How can I get my users to take better advantage of the environment?" These questions are odd as they both evidence a situation where the users and the executives were not "sold" on the data warehouse in the first place. In order to have full leverage of the environment, these are the two groups that are most responsible.

The quote for this section touched me when I first heard it. It seems funny at first and many of us can relate to it, from either the mechanic or the church angle! After the initial reaction though, the deeper truth is seen. In order to truly embrace something, you must believe in it and be willing to constantly re-invest yourself to the goal. You come to realize that everything you do is now open to interrogation and inspection. You find the faults, understand the causes, change your behavior and start the cycle anew. To embrace is not a one-time event but a change in the way you interact and react.

These next tips are all about embracing the warehouse environment and using it to the fullest possible advantage. A big part of this is that people must understand that the data warehouse is a living, evolving, ever expanding element in the information structure. While you cannot be spending money without understanding the value and payback, the warehouse environment should be looked at from the perspective that every year or so new investment will be required. The day you stop investing in the system is the day that you start to lose sight of your business.

As discussed earlier, this all comes down to a new philosophy. It is one of continual insight and exploration. The more you can get the users to embrace this mind set, the faster, and greater, your return on investment will grow.

The Data Warehouse Value Hierarchy

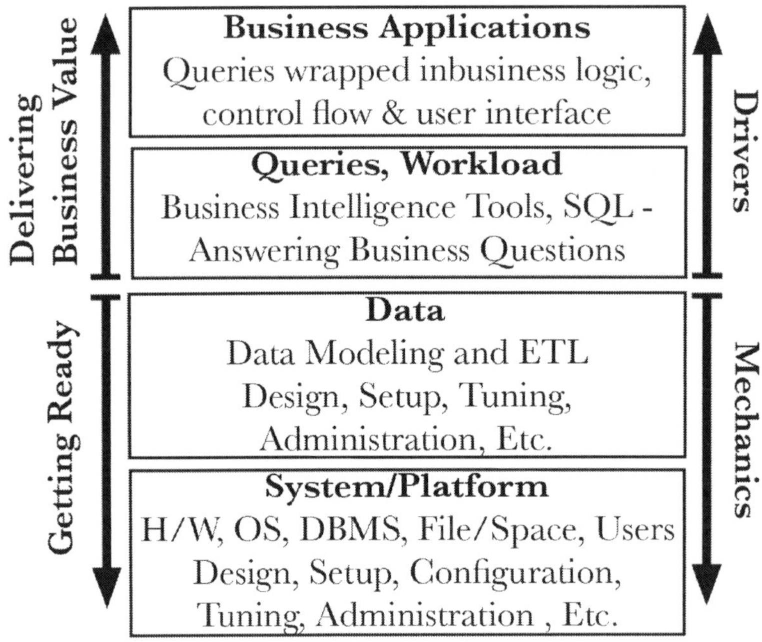

Are you spending more time assembling and maintaining the pieces or are you driving somewhere?

Those of us who have spent most of our career in the IT field have a tendency to focus on what we are building rather than why we are building it or how it will be used. We become enamored with the myriad of ways we can set up the file system, tune initialization parameters, write OS scripts, work around (or sneak around) the OS or DBMS settings, configure the hardware, etc. We are more like automobile mechanics than those who need to drive the automobile to transport a load or arrive at a different place.

To be fair, the underlying technology architecture and platform is necessary to deliver any data solution to the business. But, it is only a means to an end. The technology should never become the main issue or an inhibitor to what is most important – enabling an increasingly complex and sophisticated array of business questions and applications sharing a rich store of business data.

There is a hierarchy to providing business intelligence. At the bottom, the foundation is the platform consisting of the hardware, operating system, file system, DBMS, disk space and supporting tools and utilities. Depending on the chosen technology and the complexity of the architecture, there can be widely varying degrees of work (read: costly people, resources, and time) to setup, manage and administer these various pieces and parts.

Once the "platform" is in place and ready, then the data can be sourced and loaded. This, again, is necessary to providing any business intelligence, but it is not in itself sufficient. Providing a robust and extensive repository of data, modeled in an application-neutral manner, that can be shared across the organization is essential to maximizing the opportunities from a data warehouse. Yet having the automobile assembled and packed with luggage is not the same as driving.

Once the data is in place, it is time to let the business loose. If the underlying technology platform and data model are robust enough, tremendous business insight can be gained from a wide array of standard, previously unanticipated and increasingly complex business questions and analyses. As understanding of the data grows, applications can be developed that surround queries with business logic and processes to impact, improve and "activate" the enterprise. These top two layers in the data warehousing hierarchy are where all of the real business value is delivered. Everything before that is just getting ready.

Why do we spend so much time on what seems to be obvious? Because a surprising number of enterprises are investing far more time and resources on the bottom two layers than on the top two layers.

So how do we ensure that we are investing our most valuable resources (people and time) in those areas that have the most impact? Here are some principles to consider:

- Business First. Business needs must drive architecture and technology decisions.
- Simple, yet robust. Business is complex and will require answers to complex questions. Don't introduce complexity where it is not necessary.
- Hide technology complexity; expect business question and data complexity. Free your people resources to focus on solving business problems, not technology problems.

Action Questions

- *Has your technology or architecture become an enabler or inhibitor to evolution and data warehousing excellence?*
- *What portion of your staff is involved in delivering answers to business questions?*
- *Do the challenges and issues you face with the data warehouse primarily involve new and evolving business and data opportunities, or seemingly endless technology problems and issues?*
- *Have your users started to drive new value? Are they exploring areas of analyses previously not thought of?*

Types of Return	Cost Savings Examples	Top Line Growth Examples
Engineered In this case the ROI is well understood in advance and is essentially guaranteed if the plans are well executed. This typically results from improvements in well understood business processes.	• IT efficiency cost savings • Reduced inventory turns • Improved asset management	• New product launch • Improved marketing and customer relationship management
Intended In this case the return is a consequence of new or suspected business insight that was discovered or confirmed through use of the data warehouse and business intelligence. These cases cannot always be guaranteed in advance.	• Discovery of customer segments that have low growth potential yet are consuming services • Discovery of product and program cannibalization • Discovery of "hidden" supply chain costs	• Discovery of new customer segments • Revised profiles of high potential customers
Unexpected This case results from using the data warehouse to respond to an unanticipated event in the marketplace. Examples of these events include business crises or opportunities, competitor actions, or "acts of God" such as weather.	• Deeper knowledge of the customer base prevents a naïve and costly response to a competitor's pricing activity • Improved distribution analysis minimizes the cost impact of an unexpected winter storm	• Rapid analysis of inventory data enables the company to capitalize on an unexpected consumer "fad"

The highest return is often from actions never before anticipated or contemplated.

Maximizing the return on a data warehousing investment is primarily a business issue. The right technology is absolutely necessary, but it is not sufficient. It is like purchasing a car. The benefit is not realized until the car is used to travel somewhere or transport something. Only the business can take the data warehousing technology, loaded with data, and exploit it to improve business decisions and business processes.

The cost or investment side of the equation is usually well understood by IT. In fact, left to their own devices, many IT groups will be too focused on the cost and make decisions that severely impair the ability of the business to realize the return. So it is critical that data warehousing return or benefit be estimated, captured and recorded by the business unit leadership with IT in a supportive role. IT's responsibility will be to provide a robust, easily accessible, extensible, scalable data platform that supports the evolving variety and complexity of business questions and direct user access. IT must meet milestones, service level agreements and budgetary commitments. But it is the business that will use this incredibly powerful tool to improve business processes and decisions, discover new business insights and respond to urgent events in the marketplace.

As the business users embrace the data warehouse, it is important to capture the financial benefits. The returns from the usage of the data warehouse can take many forms. To begin with there are those that are anticipated and even controlled or "engineered." In these cases it is primarily a matter of execution. An example for a retailer would be reduced inventory turns.

But not all ROI can be "engineered" or planned. Some of the most dramatic examples of a data warehousing "return" were not anticipated when the data warehouse investment was originally made. The first category of this type of benefit is what we call "discovered" ROI. It is the return that comes as a consequence of information-driven business discovery. It might be new insights on customers or market behavior. It might be new insights on the effectiveness of business processes.

Another significant ROI opportunity is what we call unanticipated or "crisis" ROI. This is where the data warehouse becomes a critical and necessary tool to help the business respond to an unexpected event in the market. Examples may be a surprise move by a competitor, a strike by a union, a government decision or an "act of God" such as weather. When an event like this occurs, a well engineered data warehouse can become an invaluable tool for the business to understand and respond in a matter of hours – often resulting in millions of dollars of savings. The business questions that will need to be researched and answered will not have been anticipated. The data warehouse must be able to quickly handle business questions that have not been "tuned" against a schema that did not assume a certain set of business questions.

Action Questions:

- *Are you tracking and reporting estimated financial benefits for which the data warehouse is a necessary enabler?*
- *Are your data warehousing investments driven by the business or IT?*
- *If your business had an unexpected event occur, are you ready to respond instead of react?*
- *Can you identify 3 examples of value where the warehouse provided insight you had not considered important?*

You can not manage below the level you measure.

The idea that you cannot manage below the level you measure came from a visit to a retailer. There was much disbelief about the usefulness of the data warehouse as for four years the business had been trying to get a handle on item inventory turns with little success. When the business was questioned why the other projects had not been successful, it was discovered that due to technical limitation of the tool sets, they had to manage inventory at the category level.

In short, they were trying to manage item level metrics without having the ability to investigate down to item level! When they were asked why this was allowed to happen, the answer was again that they were trying to use the "standard tools", since the cost to collect, manage, and analyze the data at item level was prohibitive. The new IT manager saw what other retailers were accomplishing and wanted to bring in new tools. Whenever he tried to gain a business case for building a real data warehouse, the business was skeptical that it would ever be delivered so they would not authorize the expense.

This is a very common situation. The business defines a need and has a good business case for the project. However, the requirements get diluted in order to make phase one succeed (while planning to provide more in phase two), business users do not get what they need to drive the business case value, and the project is deemed a failure so phase two is never undertaken.

Take a good look at your business case. Does it need detailed data? Does it need data on a more frequent basis? Does it need to have data from several cross-functional areas? If so, then it is incumbent on the executive to see that barriers are removed to make this happen. Do not get fooled into thinking every tool can produce a data warehouse. If the requirements to drive the business case have been provided, then you must question the usage of the system. Are the users looking at exceptions? Are they doing deeper analysis on atomic data? How are they measuring the change in the metrics that justified the business case?

So how does this relate to users embracing the warehouse? Very simply, it is up to the users to demand the removal of barriers to success. If they do not, then they have not truly embraced the new thinking nor have they moved from "looking at things" to "looking for things." Once the users start looking for things and asking the "what if" questions, then they have embraced the new way of driving business through actionable information.

Action Questions:

- *Are your users getting what was promised?*
- *Are they starting to ask for more information?*
- *Are they starting to think and act differently?*
- *Are the users able to see, effect and create change to the metrics they are responsible for measuring?*

If you are not making decisions, then why are you asking questions?

Many projects are driven by the concept of return on investment (ROI). People want to know what are they going to get if they commit to the project and when will those rewards be seen. Many times this is measured in "hard" or quantifiable dollars. What is often overlooked are those "soft" dollars that cannot be readily determined. This is also known as lost opportunity costs.

Once the project has been authorized and implemented, people want to see those returns quantified. This is where the concept of return on actions (ROA) comes into play. As users perform analysis and make decisions, they need to capture some simple information to drive the ROA. The idea is to capture this information as part of the process, rather than undergo an arduous task of collecting the data months after the fact. The information you want to collect for each project is:

1) What analysis did you do in general business terms?
2) What actions did you take based on that analysis?
3) What benefit did you expect to see due to these actions?
4) When would these benefits be measurable?

With these data points you have integrated the ROA and ROI calculations into your business processes. People can now see and share the results of decision making. People become more responsible and accountable for these results, and the results can be directly linked to corporate objectives.

This does not need to become overbearing and cumbersome. Not every decision has to be tracked or measured. You may start off by tracking actions that are expected to produce a value of $100,000 (whatever threshold makes sense in your environment, given your investment and business case) or any action that is the result of significantly time-consuming analysis. You can also link this back to the usage reports of the system. If you notice certain users are the biggest drivers of the workload, you may ask them to capture more of the ROA data points. Start this practice and you can avoid a repeat of the following conversation we had with one company.

User: Last month we generated over 20,000 reports
Consultant: Great, what actions did those reports drive?
User: I don't know.

Either actions are not being taken, or they are not being shared. In either case the warehouse is not moving forward as quickly as it could.

Action Questions:

- *What process does your company have for linking analysis to action?*
- *How are the results of action measured, and communicated?*
- *Can you readily identify the return from five actions driven from data warehouse analysis?*

Who does – wins

It is not how often you swing the hammer, it is how often you hit the nail.

There is a law in physics that every action has an equal and opposite reaction. Taking liberties with the law you get "if every action has a reaction, which do you want to be?" In business you are either leading or you are reacting to the actions of your competitors. By embracing the data warehouse arena, you move to an environment of predicting events and therefore taking actions to control events.

This was illustrated wonderfully by the actions of Wal*Mart in the early hours and days after the September 11, 2001 New York attack. This story has been widely spread, most notably in the Wall Street Journal online version, (WSJ.Com, 9/18/2001).

The basics are that by using forecasts from previous years, Wal*Mart had stocked their stores with a limited number of American flags on September 10, 2001. As Wal*Mart tracks the inventory and sales positions in a near real time environment, they were able to see that the few thousands of flags in the stores were quickly disappearing. By understanding this and taking actions quickly, they were able to work with suppliers and increase stock. All told, they sold over 200,500 flags as opposed to approximately 10,000 the previous year.

What's more, Wal*Mart also understood the trends of the sales patterns quickly. They noticed the sales shifting from flags to other necessities like bottled water, canned foods, gas cans, guns and ammunition, and so on. Wal*Mart saw, catered to, and rode the trend. All others were constantly reacting to old news and missing every major opportunity.

Having been at the Wal*Mart headquarters in the early years of their warehouse, it is easy to understand why they capitalized so well when others did not. They have an environment that has truly encouraged and embraced the data warehouse. Many years ago they enabled and encouraged the ability to ask any question. After that they made it clear to the users that it was expected they would look "for things" rather than "at things." It does not happen easily, but it does not happen by accident either. It is the do-ers that determine the actions; the watchers can only react and constantly correct their business processes.

Action Questions:

- *What new innovations have you pioneered in your industry?*
- *Is your company seen as a leader in some area of service?*
- *How long does it take before you understand a trend happening in your business?*
- *Do you understand how external events affect your business? And are those captured in the warehouse?*
- *How well do you have visibility to those external events?*

Are you exacerbating the losses or impeding the results?

If you spend your time with trivial tasks then you never have to do anything important.
- The Phantom Tollbooth

In a classic Dilbert cartoon, the pointy-headed manager is telling the group that the current revenue slump is due to the economy. Wally cleverly observes that when revenue is up it is due to insightful business decisions but when revenues are down it was due to forces beyond our control. Does your company see the world the same way?

We have all been to, and in fact worked at, companies that succeed despite all they do to fail. The internal systems are highly silo-ed, data is completely inconsistent, reports are inaccurate, and feedback on actions is not part of the process. Yet they will still manage to eke some growth out of the market and claim victory. One only wonders how successful they could be if information systems did what they were supposed to do, i.e. provide information!

The embracement of the data warehouse means that users are actively encouraged to question the way business is run. What caused the drop in sales? Why are certain products being chosen over others? Should we even keep offering certain services? These are all examples of the type of analysis that happens when users start looking for the underlying causes to the business conditions.

At a financial institution, the comment was made that they were at the mercy of the market. One executive wanted to know that if that is true, then why do they bother to employ analysts? Clearly there are some market forces beyond your control, but even those conditions have precursors that can be spotted and then actions can be planned out to minimize the financial exposure.

The corresponding point is that there must be a measurement component to the environment. If actions are not contributing as expected, then make refinements. This is the fail fast philosophy. Make decisions, take actions, measure them for effectiveness, and then refine as necessary. A side aspect to this philosophy is that the users also need to understand how their actions affect other functions in the company. Do you have groups that are effectively canceling out each other's efforts?

This is best shown with a discussion we had with a retail company a few years ago. After discussing the positive change the data warehouse could bring, a high-ranking audience member raised a challenge. He said, "We are currently growing at over 15% per year, so how can you say that we are not doing well?" We then asked, "What is keeping you from growing at over 20% per year." His silence made the point. When the users just accept the situation and are unwilling to question the processes, answers, or actions, then the warehouse is not being embraced. One must embrace change; it is the only constant in business.

Action Questions:

- *How well do your business units understand the overall impact to their decisions?*
- *What are the five biggest obstacles you face in moving your business forward? How can data analysis help overcome those obstacles?*
- *Does everyone understand how their job and decisions affect the overall health of the company?*

We went from looking *at* things,
to looking *for* things.

All great data warehouse projects have examples where business users embraced the opportunity, made discoveries about their business and used that new insight to deliver significant ROI. There is the mutual funds company that modified its premiere client profile after studying the previously unavailable account transaction detail in its new data warehouse. There are the retailers who uncovered employee fraud through new detail data in the data warehouse. Often the most powerful discoveries from data are found by business users who dive into the data.

Nationwide is a major Midwest insurance company covering 16 million policies across auto, home, life and commercial and including asset management and annuities. Nationwide manages over $117 billion in statutory assets.

The business users at Nationwide Insurance are continually uncovering new ways to improve their business through the use of their data warehouse. According to the data warehousing team, they knew the data warehouse was there to stay when the business users began "knocking down the doors" trying to get access to the data warehouse. To ensure that the business units are continually driving the priorities and evolution of the data warehouse Nationwide formed not only a data warehouse steering committee but also a Business Advisory Team (BAT). Following is a brief description of the role of the BAT at Nationwide:

Representation from core functions of the business:
Product, Operations, Claims, Sales, Finance and Marketing

- Provides business requirements and drives individual releases
- Represents functional perspectives while establishing cross-functional benefits
- Ensures the projected Business Value/ROI is realized from the initiative
- Establishes priorities based on warehouse strategies and future vision

Nationwide also works hard at promoting the data warehouse. Examples of this are:

- Conducting quarterly "lunch and learns" where actual business sponsors demo their application and business value to a cross-functional audience.
- Conducting Data Warehouse expos at least once a year where all business sponsors have a booth to educate others on their applications.
- Highlighting data warehouse successes within internal company publications.
- Working with the business sponsors to partner on submissions for Industry Award recognition.

- Creating a data warehouse logo and 'catch phrase' for inclusion on reports and projects that were enabled by the data warehouse. This promotes recognition of the data warehouse value.

Nationwide has also implemented a solid training program required for all users requesting access to the warehouse. Although the training does provide an overview of the technology and tool fundamentals, it focuses primarily on the foundational data and inherent data relationships. This training must be completed before access is granted. Pre-requisites for this training are sent out prior to the class and must be completed. This helps Nationwide maximize their time on the data training that is instrumental in the discovery of the new business insight.

Nationwide has numerous examples of how the business has been able to leverage the data warehouse, often in a manner not necessarily anticipated when the data warehouse was originally conceived. In one example the business users were able to reevaluate policies using the much greater detail available to them in their new data warehouse. Using this new detail they were able to make premium adjustments and better manage their risk! In another example, special investigative units in the field are able to mine the data warehouse for alerts. In one case they found they were supposedly insuring Harley Davidson motorcycles when in fact the bikes were frauds having been built from parts. They were able to research and cross compare vehicle identification numbers and other identifiers to find the fakes.

Additionally, current efforts surrounding their CRM activity within the marketing organization have resulted in over $6 million of new premiums to date. All of this was possible because Nationwide business users are embracing the data warehouse and associated tools.

And Nationwide is never satisfied. At least once each year they meet to review and evolve their data warehousing strategy. Are there more opportunities to use data in the enterprise? Will more data sources, greater data accessibility, more timely data, for example, provide greater opportunities for ROI?

Are your business users aggressively embracing the data warehouse? Are they looking for new opportunities to leverage the information? If not, what opportunities are you missing? If so, are you building on what you have achieved?

Extending

If you've got it, flaunt it.

Once the user community has embraced the data warehouse, strategic analysis will begin to drive real results. Measurements are now understood, actions can be linked to value, and the timeframe between making a decision and seeing a return starts to shrink. As this happens, it is a natural consequence that the data warehouse starts to move from the strategic to the tactical environment.

By this stage of the evolution, data quality has been questioned and is being addressed where necessary. Users and executives are now starting to look for the next wave. The next area that can dramatically raise the return of investment in the warehouse arena is integration with operational systems.

One of the barriers to moving data to a more frequent, more detailed, or more cross functional capability is the legacy system. The data is only as good, or as timely, as the feeder systems that provide the information. In the past it was not cost-effective to try to change the legacy systems to increase the frequency or depth of data loads. As the users tap the potential of the existing data warehouse, the input of the data is now up for review, and can be justified from a business perspective.

The purview of the system now must extend and address the operational and legacy systems. This is a major attitude and cultural change, in the past such a connection was prohibited and deemed dangerous. This attitude meant that the business had to forever live with a time lag between when an event happened and when a strategy was applied to it.

There are two types of examples to illustrate this point. The first is removing the time lag between the event and the action. You want to get the data being generated from your operational systems into your data warehouse as soon as possible. Many companies are either already at, or moving rapidly toward the point where data is in the warehouse within an hour of the event. A handful of companies have the data within minutes. This means that actions can be taken on events when the impact is highest.

Another aspect of this idea is the removal of the time barriers to taking action on data that has been collected. In this vein, triggers are set to apply actions as events happen.

One good example of this type of thinking is in the promotion and marketing arena. In the past, companies would take actions (send out a promotion) in the hopes of generating an event (a sale). Now companies are looking at events (a sale of an item) and creating actions (a targeted promotion for a related item).

Companies are always coming up with great "promotions." One such idea would be low cost telephone billing. A promotion is run for people that sign up in the next 30 days to get 5 cents a minute billing. What about your existing customers? What about the customers that you will attract? What impact does this have on your networks and cost structures? A better way of running the business is to segment your customers and prospects so that when they fit a certain profile they get the better billing arrangement. As an existing customer I should not have to re-apply or constantly watch for special deals. If my calling patterns show I am a good customer, then give me the good rate automatically.

Some companies are already doing this. Others have stuck with the "trolling" method. The main indication of this stage of evolution is that the strategic decisions that you make are ingrained into the operational tactical decision-making process. You can think of it as being "during the fact" instead of "after the fact."

Action Questions:

- *Is your warehouse seen as only a strategic tool or do operational decisions get made from the data as well?*
- *What operational decision can be supported from the data you currently possess?*
- *What is the time lag between your operational and informational environments?*

Old thinking: Strategy versus Tactics,
New Thinking: Tactics encompass Strategy

Seize, keep and exploit the initiative.
- John R. Elting

The business cycle has churned many times in the past few decades and the pendulum continues to swing. In particular you get different sides arguing whether the company has to be more focused on the short-term tactical functions or the longer-term strategic direction of the company. As most successful businesses understand, there is not a decision whether to do one or the other. The business must decide how the two sides complement one another and how they can both be deployed simultaneously.

The commonality between the two environments is the data. Data from the tactical, day to day operational systems are used to drive analysis, which in turn determines the longer-term strategy. Then when the strategy is deployed, the actions drive new data to be collected or incorporated into the analysis.

In order to bring the two philosophies together you must first bring the data together. Now more than ever though, it means physically tying the data feeds and the strategic analysis together in a close knit loop that encompasses the feedback of actions to refined analysis.

This is a radical concept for many people, because now the line between decision support and operational systems blurs. However, when one thinks about what is happening during this evolution, you are just fine-tuning the decision making process to the point of near real time (or real timely as we like to say) interactions.

In this situation, your company can rapidly decide if the customer on the phone should be treated differently due to interaction within the last few hours. Did they recently call in a complaint and yet their name is on your outbound marketing "to-call" list? Most likely they are not in the mood to make additional purchases from you. Quickly take their names off the marketing lists for the immediate future. Sometimes the best way to recognize the customer is to leave them alone!

Action Questions:

- *Do your short term tactical actions support your long-term strategy or are they "triage without any thought to surgery?"*
- *When making operational or tactical decision, do your users support those decisions with empirical data or gut instinct?*
- *Do your systems support getting the necessary information in a time effective manner?*
- *Do you understand your total customer view up to the last interaction they had with you, regardless of the venue?*
- *Do you have "action without analysis" or "analysis without action"?*

Flying by wire

Set your intentions and let the system alert you
to the turbulence of your business.

There is a term called "flying by wire" which means the pilots do not actually fly the plane all the time. If you are flying into San Diego, the pilot inputs the destination code for San Diego into the computer and flight paths, speeds, and such are calculated based on a variety of factors.

The interesting point about this is that when the plane encounters an unusual situation, such as turbulence, it does not know the best way to handle the exception. In these cases the pilot needs to take command of the plane and resolve the situation. Of course what we all prefer is that the computer be constantly tracking other variables and conditions. Rather than being surprised about the turbulence, we are notified well in advance of the situation. Here the pilot can make minor corrections to the flight plan and fly around the problem area without the passengers being any wiser.

This is how you want your business to operate. You want to have the majority of your operations and business on autopilot. Look at your processes and procedures. Do you have manual intervention for a wide variety of decisions that are routine. If you are generating reports, look at the actions those reports spawn. How many of them could be automated? Embed your business practices into the data to trigger actions automatically. You also want to have the exceptions trigger warning flags so intelligent humans can look at the situation and resolve it the best possible way. Better yet, you want to set those warning flags back far enough in your process that your end customers are never affected by the problem.

The classic example here is inventory. It is easy to get reports about out of stock inventory. It is also easy to understand what the solution is: reorder the product. Most retailers have figured out lead times and sales patterns enough to actually have the idea of safety stock. This is the amount of product necessary on hand when the re-ordering takes place. This is setting the flags in advance of the problem and letting the computer do the work. But what if your supplier went on strike? Then you need to intervene and have people re-allocate the remaining inventory most effectively to your stores. This is an exception and it is what you want to be dealing with for success. Get the routine automated and get your intelligent resources focusing on the real issues.

Action Questions:

- *What routine decisions are made from the data in the warehouse?*
- *Can they be automated to some degree?*
- *What other actions have been automated off the data warehouse in your company?*
- *How far back are you setting the flags to understand and respond to turbulence?*
    - *Are your users looking for the needle in a haystack of data or are important exceptions being presented to them automatically?*

Thought is sad without action,
and action is sad without thought.
- Henri Amiel

As you begin linking strategic decision making with action taking, there are many ways to make missteps. One area is that many people start to confuse the act of being efficient in their processes with being effective in their actions.

For example, with the introduction of e-coupons and e-mail marketing, companies can now send out mailings and promotions for a fraction of the cost. Unfortunately, this does not increase the likelihood people will respond to your promotions, and in fact it may actually lower your response rates. The fact that it was highly efficient does not help the business drive new revenue (though one can argue that at least you lost less money).

As you make the linkage between the two environments, you want to move to being more effective with your marketing. Go ahead and send the 4-color brochure, but only send it to those individuals that will respond with a 85% probability. Reduce the cost of the promotion by decreasing waste and as a result, increase the business value with highly targeted understanding.

Many people can argue that this falls into the "embracing" section, but there is one more piece to this situation. The real goal is to move from being effective to efficacious, which is the convergence of effective and efficient! Now you are making use of highly targeted and highly segmented decisions in a near real time case. Think of reseating your best frequent flyers when the airplane is delayed. Think of prioritizing the routing of call centers based on true customer value as opposed to rough monthly scorings. The more you can use all your resources to drive higher profitability in the near term, the more you can impact results.

Another aspect of the convergence is that as you start to drive action into a triggered process, you need to have the process assume a factor of human learning. For example, in a travel booking situation, it is not enough to know that your customer prefers a seat in the front sections of the plane. Maybe they prefer that only on short flights or on segments where they have to make connections. On longer flights, such as international ones, maybe the preference is for seats at the back where the likelihood of having several seats together are greater (and the customer can stretch out more). These are the types of considerations we used to expect from a dedicated travel agent. In the extended data warehouse, this intelligence needs to be somehow replicated.

Action Questions:

- *Are you simply streamlining your processes or making your processes more intelligent?*
- *As you move to automated action, have you instituted human learning into your automation?*

The real test, are you changing "business as usual?"

Success seems to be connected with action.
Successful people keep moving.
They make mistakes, but they don't quit.
- Conrad Hilton

In his book, Of Paradise and Power, Robert Kagan explains the geopolitical environment of the U.S. and Europe. He states that when people do not have the ability to resolve a problem, they not only become tolerant to the problem, but actually start to deny its existence. This thought is followed up with a corollary of sorts. Those who have the ability to resolve problems, start looking for larger problems to solve.

As you extend the data warehouse, you can see this idea played out in the business world as well. When executives and users cannot get answers, there is a cycle of crisis and eventual acceptance of the "way business is." Companies that have successfully evolved the data warehouse arena do not accept "business as usual." They constantly look to see where the next opportunity can be found. Are you losing margin from inventory shrinkage? Are your cashiers not as productive as they could be? Should different people be on different shifts? Are your resources allocated as well as possible?

When you ask these questions to people who cannot get analysis in a timely fashion or to users who have not embraced action-based decisioning, they question the impact such areas could have on the total bottom line. When you have extended the warehouse, you come to understand that any movement in your metrics can have potentially huge benefits.

This is best seen by looking at companies who do not stop questioning their processes and the ways in which other entities affect those processes. As you open the warehouse to external users, be it your suppliers, partners, or customers, you are getting the maximum return on your investments and taking the company to a new level of business.

Action Questions:

- *Do your external partners have access to your data environment? Is their access as free as security and privacy allows?*
- *What data in the warehouse is available to help streamline or understand your operational processes?*
- *Can you identify what are the largest gaps or drains in your processes?*

The Extending Case study

Mankind is divided into three classes – the immovable, the movable, and those who move.
- Arab saying

3M has a very sophisticated data warehouse environment. Here the data warehouse started out with the basic information and decision support. The system quickly expanded to include a truly global enterprise environment with users from around the globe having access to a centralized system. Once it was apparent that the data warehouse was a good system of record, operational usage was envisioned. As the data warehouse had a consistent product list, sales inventory, vendor information and such, 3M introduced operational applications such as web pages and call center support.

This provided the entire company, and many external sources such as retailers and end customers, with accurate, timely, and consistent information. Most importantly, it started leveraging the environment in ways previously thought impossible. In particular, opening the environment to the web site so users could ask their own questions without having to use the call center was particularly helpful. Just as the phone company made us all operators and banks have made us all tellers, 3M is making us all call center employees!

Now people will say that this is not necessarily a data warehouse application, as many companies have opened information to customers via the web site. While this is true, the important aspect is that 3M has followed the philosophy of bringing data together and then letting process come to data rather than driving data to process. While the look up of information is not a classic data warehouse application, the fact the data in the warehouse is being leveraged shows how the idea of a "single face" is being played out by 3M.

Finally, the impact this extension of the data warehouse has had is in the neighborhood of $1,000,000 per week in reduced call center workload. This does not even include the operational efficiency of reduced data redundancy and management.

In a similar vein, a grocery chain has extended the usage of their data warehouse to include alerting the store managers of problems by tracking the sales patterns of key items. For example, if milk does not sell within a 15-minute window then there is a high probability of a problem. Milk could be out of stock, or there is a blocked dairy case or some other issue. In any event the store manager is alerted to the situation for investigation and resolution. Again, this is not your classic usage of a data warehouse, but it is a very good leverage of the data that is already being collected for other reasons.

Entanglements – Common Missteps To Avoid

The first rule of holes:
When you're in one, stop digging.
- Molly Ivins

If you look in the library you will notice hundreds of books on how to succeed in many different ventures. You may be surprised to find that there are no books on how to fail. The reason for this is that failure is easy. Thousands of people are failing every day. There is no trick to it. To fail all you need to do is not have a goal you believe in, not be willing to ask the tough questions of your plan, or be willing to hear the tough answers to those questions.

However, it is also true that if you do not study history then you are condemned to repeat it. We would love to claim that every data warehousing project is wildly successful and delivers clear and significant business value. Alas, this is far from the truth. From time to time, "experts" have offered their opinion as to the number or percentage of data warehousing "failures." We will not attempt any such assertions. Even if everyone did agree on a definition of success or failure, it is impossible to gather accurate statistics (since few of us are willing to expose our missteps.)

We believe data warehousing success should only be assessed in terms of business impact: significant, continuous, expanding and often rapid business impact. We know that it can be successful.

Data warehousing excellence is about doing things right, or as some have suggested, doing the right thing right. But it is also important to not do certain things: do not head down certain paths; do not paint yourself into a corner; do not become entangled in a briar patch.

In this section we will look at what we consider some of the common pitfalls in data warehousing. They may not cause a data warehousing project to fail, but they will certainly limit, delay or prevent its success. In all cases they will significantly increase the cost of a data warehousing effort.

After reviewing these entanglements, take a look at your own situation. If some of these are familiar, it is best to take the time to address them. As we have often learned, good enough is neither. Don't settle for second rate and you won't end up with a second rate solution.

The IT/Business Disconnect

Similarity of outlook creates friendship.
- Democritus

The following two entanglements we discuss are related. They stem from the disconnect that sometimes occurs between IT and the business groups they serve.

Before we discuss these particular issues, we want to be clear that many IT organizations have provided tremendous leadership in data warehousing and decision support. They have become the change agents and made possible what the business users thought was unattainable. A key component of what makes these IT organizations successful is the strong partnership they have forged with the business organizations and the trust they have developed. Yet it has not always gone well.

We know of a telecommunications company that had invested heavily in data warehousing. In fact, it was considered a leader in data warehousing during the mid-1990s. They had implemented a complex hub and spoke environment with numerous data marts. They had moved from one platform to the next and had nearly 200 people on their data warehousing and business intelligence team in IT. Yet with all this, the business units were still frustrated. In their view, IT had failed to address their needs. Some business groups were investigating outsourcing opportunities to have their decision support needs met. The relationship was extremely hostile and dysfunctional. Yet these were bright, sincere, hard working, well meaning people. They cared deeply about their company. But somehow there had been a huge disconnect.

IT professionals and business professionals have different skills, different biases, different goals and different measurements. They approach decision support and data warehousing systems from different places, with different perspectives. With typical process-oriented applications, this gap between business needs and IT can be negotiated and captured in detailed business requirements, system requirements and system design, and verified in careful and in depth testing. This works because these applications automate business processes that are well understood and relatively stable.

But decision support is fundamentally different. It is inherent in decision support that the needs of the business are constantly evolving. Requirements are rarely stable. Often there is no time for lengthy and involved requirements development, design and tuning processes. Unlike typical applications, the business users can interact directly with the data, and numerous business rule layers and cumbersome processes should not separate them. For this reason it is imperative that there be a close, dynamic, working partnership between the business and IT.

Avoiding the Tar Pits

- *Establish a strong, collaborative partnership between the business users and IT.*
- *Create an overlapping organization consisting of IT and business personnel with shared objectives and accountability for the successful evolution of data warehouse and decision support system value.*
- *Create an executive steering and oversight committee consisting of senior Business and IT management.*
- *Develop relevant Service Level Agreements based on reasonable business needs. Expect these to change. Periodically review and modify them.*
- *Jointly assess data warehouse progress and value by identifying the business benefits received.*
- *Celebrate successes together (business and IT).*

It is not enough to take steps which may some day lead to a goal; each step must itself be a goal and a step likewise.
– Goethe

As data warehousing became popular in the 1990s, many IT organizations saw an opportunity to regain control of corporate data assets and clean up years of corporate data issues. This was and continues to be a tremendous opportunity for data warehousing. But too often the emphasis was on the data warehouse and its underlying technology as an end in itself.

When a well meaning IT organization sets out to implement a data warehouse without clear business objectives, priorities and partnerships, they inevitably stall, fall short of expectations, and struggle to justify the investment. Furthermore, there are often ill-advised architecture and technology decisions that preclude the eventual success of the data warehouse as they are not based on driving defined business opportunities.

In their defense, IT will argue, "But the business users cannot tell us what they want! They always want it sooner than we can deliver. When they begin to use what we deliver, even when it is what they asked for, they change their minds."

You will certainly get no argument from us! We have been there many times. Sometimes data warehousing and decision support system projects are like the blind leading the blind. Often both the business and IT are venturing into new territory together. Even so, the business will usually have a better sense of what will have a valuable impact.

In cases where IT recognizes the opportunity and desires to move forward, it is imperative that they encourage the business organizations into a leadership role. IT may drive, but the business should be determining the next step on the journey and navigating along the way. To assist the business with catching the vision, IT can sponsor business management attendance at user group meetings or seminars or arrange reference calls with other organizations that have already realized the benefits of data warehousing.

Avoiding the Tar Pits

- *Always begin with business objectives. These should be largely defined by the users.*
- *Evolve the IT infrastructure under the umbrella of evolving business solutions. This may require rework and some additional cost but over time much more business value will be delivered while avoiding the cost of failure.*
- *Never design a data warehouse infrastructure "from the bottom up." You don't begin with the hardware and OS and then proceed upwards through the IT "stack." Rather, you should begin with the long term business vision for the DSS environment and the near term goals and make IT architecture and technology decisions based on those business needs.*

- *Expect business needs and direction to change. Design for simplicity and flexibility. As IT delivers capability to the business it will open their eyes to new opportunities.*
- *Assess progress frequently by identifying the business benefits received.*
- *In the case where the business does not yet see the value of data warehousing, don't over promise in the beginning. Deliver a steady stream of straightforward and relatively simple capabilities while building trust. Then be prepared to grow and move rapidly as the users catch on and momentum builds.*
- *You may not know exactly what they want, but you do know what they need. Unfettered access to a set of integrated, consistent business data. Make sure that is not inhibited along the way.*

Caution: Business Units at the Wheel

Hell hath no greater fury than a vested interest masquerading as a moral principle.

- Barber Conable

Lest anyone think from the previous chapter that we see most of the data warehousing issues existing with IT, this is not the case. Yes, there are risks and pitfalls if a data warehousing effort is solely an IT-driven initiative. Yet there are also issues and risks if a business unit is driving the effort without strong involvement on the part of IT.

The most common pitfall we encounter when a business unit is driving the data warehousing effort is that the design and use of the data warehouse is tailored for the needs of that business unit, to the exclusion of other business units. Eventually the tremendous opportunities from cross-functional data sharing are lost. Although the initial phases of a data warehouse may focus on the needs of a particular business unit, the architecture and design should reflect a long term enterprise wide exploitation of the data warehouse.

Another concern is that people on the business side rarely appreciate the tremendous challenges of sourcing, transforming and normalizing data and managing it in a manner that can be most effective. These data sourcing challenges are especially difficult during the first 12-18 months of a data warehousing project. It is important that business people understand the complexities of these issues. If they have patience, the issues will be resolved and the data quality and robustness continuously improved.

It is also easy for business people to become enamored with slick looking front end tools and pre-built applications that promise more than they can deliver. Front end tools and applications are the doors and windows to the house, not the foundation. Regardless how attractive the doors and windows, they mean nothing if the foundation is not solid.

Data warehousing is not magic. There is an incredible amount of work that is occurring in the system to answer even simple business questions. What would appear to be very simple changes to a business question or a data schema can have a tremendous impact on the amount of work the system needs to perform. The amount of work performed by the system can be very different when asking a question using a qualifier of "X AND Y" rather than "X OR Y." It is not necessary for the business person to understand the subtleties of how the system operates, but they should know that these situations exist and they work closely with their IT counterparts to understand the implications of asking a question a certain way.

As we have said many times before, the most successful data warehousing efforts exist when there is a strong partnership between the business users and IT. Together they share responsibility for the evolving success of the data warehouse.

Avoiding the Tar Pits

- *Establish a cross organizational team including multiple business units and IT to own the data warehouse.*
- *Develop a reasonable, phased implementation plan which allows for learning along the way. Understand that it takes months and even years to establish a robust data repository. Value can be delivered in stages while the underlying foundation is continuously improved.*
- *Take time to allow the IT personnel to explain why certain activities will require more time and resources. You may save yourself some frustration by phrasing a business question a bit differently.*
- *Early on the priority must be to get a solid foundation. It may not be that broad, but it must be robust. Front end tools won't solve issues with inadequate or poor quality data.*

If one takes care of the means, the end will take of itself.
- Mohandas Ghandi

Establishing clear expectations is fundamental to any healthy relationship. Service Level Agreements (SLAs) can be a powerful tool for the business user to capture, codify and communicate expectations and priorities to IT. But as Albert Einstein once said, "Not everything that can be counted counts and not everything that counts can be counted."

Typical SLAs are often based on system availability and system performance. These are easy to measure. But when emphasized out of context, they can drive inappropriate behavior and ill-advised decisions. One of our colleagues heard an IT professional declare that they have great performance in their data warehouse – they never allow a query to run longer than five seconds! Another IT group improved system availability by removing direct user access to the data warehouse.

SLAs need to be defined around relevance to the business. Data accessibility is more relevant than system availability. Data freshness and data quality may be more important than system response time. The ability to get an answer to a single business question in a few hours may be more important than being able to answer that same question in 5 seconds if I have to wait 3 weeks for IT to implement the "tuned" query.

Combine these DSS-oriented SLAs with other measures of IT effectiveness such as adding new subject data areas, providing more powerful analytical tools and meeting milestones and you will ensure a decision support environment that is not only more useful but constantly improving.

Avoiding the Tar Pits

- *Define Service Level Agreements in the areas of data freshness, data quality, data accessibility, and data criticality.*
- *Define Service Level Agreements that are tied to evolution and improvement of the data warehouse.*
- *Balance SLAs with other management objectives such as on time and on budget delivery of commitments.*

Smart People Overcomplicating Simple Architectures

A society which scorns excellence in plumbing because plumbing is a humble activity and tolerates shoddiness in philosophy because it is an exalted activity will have neither good plumbing nor good philosophy.
- John Gardner

A few years ago, one of us had assumed responsibility for the computing architecture of a Fortune 500 company. He was handed an IT blueprint that had been developed by one of the major systems integrators. The opening premise of this blueprint was along the following lines (paraphrased):

"Today's dynamic business environment is extremely complex and constantly changing. Successful companies will require IT infrastructures that can service this complex, ever-changing environment. Thus, these IT infrastructures must be complex and ever changing...." We disagree.

A decision support environment must be extremely responsive to real world complexity and change, for that is the only way that the business can respond to events. In order to do this, the data warehousing infrastructure must have simplicity, robustness and flexibility to provide a stabilizing influence.

We in IT are essentially the automotive engineers and mechanics for the IT infrastructure. Since we are not the drivers of the vehicle, we can place far too much importance on the myriad of clever ways to assemble the parts than pursuing our true mission: to provide a robust, reliable, easy to use, multi-use vehicle for the drivers of the business.

Simple architectures lead to greater flexibility. Complex architectures encumber flexibility and evolution. Decision support and data warehousing, especially as it extends throughout the enterprise and beyond, will have necessary complexity at the various data model and application layers. Yet to enable the combination of complexity and flexibility it is critical that the underlying information system architecture be kept as simple as possible.

Throughout the environment, you want to minimize the number of places where change will cause problems. Were your loads designed to be run at night? That will need to change when users need more frequent data. Are the tuning parameters dependent on the number of users? That will need to change as you add new business groups. Was your data distributed based on volume or usage? That will change with growth and new analysis. The paradox is that a more complex plan usually leads to a less elegant, and less flexible, solution.

Avoiding the Tar Pits

- *Strive for simplicity in the underlying platform architecture, such as integrated layers and a minimal number of physical platforms.*
- *Only allow complexity where it is necessary to deliver business value such as the lowest level atomic data where the admittedly complex normalized data model is necessary to support the evolving business needs.*
- *Keep "auxiliary" data structures to a minimum, especially if they are used to improve system performance. By auxiliary we mean the myriad of*

denormalized data structures often implemented such as summary tables and indexes.

- *Keep Extract, Transformation and Load (ETL) processes as simple and straightforward as possible. Avoid DBMS technologies that necessitate complexity in the ETL logic and processes. The additional complexity in these processes again inhibits flexibility and evolution along with increased design, implementation, maintenance and processing costs.*
- *Avoid data marts unless there is no other means of addressing an important business need. The additional hardware, software and networking platform components again increase cost and impact the ability to evolve the system.*

Death by A Thousand Cuts -
Stubborn Pursuit of a Flawed Technology Decision

It was a bad plan flawlessly executed.

Both of us have witnessed, and at least one of us has personally experienced what can be called the Total Cost of Failure. Total Cost of Failure is the consequence of missed milestones, lost business opportunities, and sacrificed business requirements. These lead to additional staff including expensive consultants, various hardware upgrades, "scaffolding software" to shore up an inadequate technology and a general loss of morale all due to an unwise and usually ill-informed technology decision. For those companies that are eventually successful in their data warehousing, there is the cost of changing horses in mid-stream. "Time is money."

Consider the most expensive component of a data warehouse – the people. Architects, designers, data base administrators, data modelers, operators, application developers, end users. Assume that the burdened, annual cost for a full time equivalent (FTE) is $100,000. (This makes the numbers easy!) For an aggregate support staff of 10 people this works out to $1M/year in personnel costs. For those of you that think you are saving money by doing a number of small data marts, thorough analysis will reveal that the actual support staff is much larger. In aggregate you could easily be investing $5M per year or far more on your staffing. We know of one European company that had 65 people managing its four data marts and a U.S. firm with nearly 200 people supporting a complex hub and spoke environment with over two dozen data marts.

Now, if someone has chosen an inadequate technology and is forced to "make it work" what happens? A 6-month schedule slip for a 10 person team costs $500K. What about a one year slip? What about the unanticipated need to double the staff? Now they are spending $1M more per year than planned.

If they decide that they will force the business users to live with the technology decision and adjust their requirements and expectations appropriately, what happens to the original business case? They are now spending $1M/year for what?

A few years ago a large American firm had undertaken a strategic corporate data warehouse initiative. Expectations were set. Promises were made to the business. The data warehouse vision was being shared at user and industry conferences. Vendor claims and promises were trusted and accepted at face value – after all, they were the strategic IT partners. Because of the political weight behind this decision, proofs of concept were performed, yet short-changed, and references were not thoroughly investigated. It was considered career limiting to challenge the decision.

But the chosen technology was clearly not adequate for the task and three years later the project had not delivered on the commitments. Some would say it had failed. The business users were extremely frustrated and refused to relinquish their older system which was continuing to deliver value. They had become cynical. Performance and availability for the new system were a joke in the organization (although not in the presence of the key decision makers). System availability was below 85%. There was plenty of finger pointing. Eventually, outside experts were brought in to audit the situation and offer recommendations. These recommendations resulted in moving the end users to redundant data marts and implementing burdensome and overly restrictive change management. Eventually this company's corporate data warehouse became a mere shadow of those implemented by their peers.

To be fair, failure is not easy to recognize. It is an admirable quality to stick with a decision and gut it out once it is made. Second guessers, nay-sayers and unbelievers can sabotage even the best decisions. How do you know that the next release won't make everything better – isn't that what the vendors will tell you?

At the same time, the stubborn pursuit of a flawed decision can cost many times more than the initial cost estimates. The end result can fail to deliver any significant value to the business. We know of one company that invested $30M over a three year period to deliver a decisions support system that was rejected by the business because it would not support their basic needs. They had attempted to use the same technology that had served them well with their operational systems but it was the wrong technology for the decision support environment.

So how do you know when it is time to change horses? (This should be apparent within the first six months of a project.)

- When milestones continually slip because of technology issues.
- When requirements become sacrificed because of technology issues.
- When the vendor who said it would stand behind you and promised that the technology could do the job starts to make excuses or admits that it is "pioneering" in a new arena along with you.
- When the support costs (people and software) have doubled while the delivered requirements have been halved.
- When you need to double the size of your system in the first 6 months while simultaneously backing away from requirements and expectations.

Avoiding the Tar Pits

- *First, recognize that data warehousing is a strategic and expensive endeavor. It is not an experiment. This is not a place to "play" with technology that has not already been proven to deliver in the marketplace.*
- *Do not take vendor claims at face value. Thoroughly investigate many references. Attend user groups (real user groups, not the marketing events offered by some vendors.)*
- *Talk to industry analysts – those whose funding comes from customers, not vendors.*
- *Perform robust, real world benchmarks or "Proof of Concepts" that stress the technology and test where you want to be rather than where you are today. Do not "dumb down' the tests in order to allow a particular vendor to compete. If you don't force out the issues and weaknesses before you begin, you will suffer from them later.*

Broken Relationships

It is the relationships between data,
not the data itself,
that gives information, insight and value.

The greatest insight and intelligence from a decision support system is derived from the relationships inherent in the data between business objects or data entities. Asking questions about "things" (customers, products, suppliers, employees, stores, etc.) can help you understand what is happening. Asking questions about the relationships between them (customers/products, products/suppliers, etc.) can help you understand why it is happening and better predict what will happen.

The relationships between business objects are varied and complex. Take customers and products for example. Customers inquire about products, they receive products, they use products, they request service on products and sometimes they return products. Customers can be related to other customers in various ways. The same is true of products with other products. These are only two very basic data entities.

Furthermore these relationships can change over time. Customers come and go. Primary suppliers are replaced by backup suppliers. Products are discontinued or modified.

The relationships and their relative importance to the business change over time. Relationships that were once considered unworthy of attention jump to the fore when a company's competitors "change the rules" or when government directives or laws place greater emphasis on information previously considered less important.

Data relationships are extremely important. Yet we often see design decisions, or worse yet, widely advocated design approaches that break or prevent the investigation of these relationships. For example:

- Dimensional modeling approaches oversimplify the varied and complex relationships inherent in the data. Although they can be very useful for certain applications and views of the data, if they become the sole data modeling approach then considerable opportunities for business intelligence will be lost.
- Subject data areas can often elevate the importance of the data entities to the neglect of the data relationships.
- Unwillingness to share data prevents many corporations from gaining the insight inherent in the relationships between data. There is much to be learned by associating operations data with product data with marketing data, etc.
- Data marts are the worst example of breaking relationships. This is because the implementation time and investment for the data mart has made it all the more difficult to rapidly adapt it for integration with other data. Change becomes an order of magnitude more expensive so change does not happen.

Avoiding the Tar Pits

- *Always start from a Third Normal Form (3NF) data model. Not all 3NF models will adequately address the data relationships but they are easier to evolve and adapt.*
- *Use technology that excels at handling complex joins and ad hoc queries. If the technology is limited, if it is painful to exploit more complex data relationships, then business opportunities will be lost.*
- *Use a single, integrated schema. It will evolve. It may have multiple "layers." But breaking it vertically into physically separate subject data areas will break relationships.*
- *Use virtual data marts and views wherever possible to insulate the end users from the complex, underlying 3NF model. Virtual data marts and views are much faster, much easier and much less expensive to implement. Thus, adapting them to the evolving business needs and underlying data model is not an issue. If you must use physically separate data marts because the desired tool is fundamentally different technology (e.g. cubes vs. relational) then create dependent data marts.*

Mistaking Real Time for Real Timely

Good and quickly seldom meet.
- George Herbert

Here is another scenario that we have seen more times than we should. An IT professional says, "With partitioning we can now append each month's data in a matter of seconds! Previously it took hours." Business Professional, "But it is at least a week after month end before I see the data. I don't see the results of our early June marketing campaign until mid-July!"

Data freshness is a growing issue in data warehousing. The recent emphasis on tactical and active data warehousing has highlighted the need to provide critical decision support information closer in time to the origination of an event.

We know of a company where the Marketing organization was attempting to use billing data to understand the impact of their marketing campaigns. This billing data included summaries of product usage and was the only indicator of customer behavior available to the Marketing department. This billing data was not available until at least 2 weeks after month end. The data was not available until the books had closed and final "adjustments" had been made. Then the data was extracted and loaded through long processes into a sequence of database systems with the last one being the decision support system used by Marketing. If they initiated a marketing campaign during the first week of July, they did not have visibility into its effectiveness until the middle of August! Yet there was great consternation when the final load processes would occasionally run 2 or 3 hours longer than normal.

Here are real examples where true timeliness in data has a huge business impact:

- Sales ticket data is in the data warehouse and used in DSS queries less than 10 minutes after the customer transaction is complete.
- Phone service changes or drops are reflected in the data warehouse within the hour and used to initiate customer profitability analysis and churn risk.
- Weather related flight cancellations are reflected in an airlines' data warehouse within minutes initiating retention incentives, alternative routes and possibly special accommodation coupons for high value frequent flyers.
- Credit card transactions are fed into the data warehouse within minutes of a transaction and compared with past buying patterns, transaction location, balance history, customer profitability and other key factors to perform fraud analysis and contact the potentially at risk client.

The challenge is often that the data warehouse only receives the data after it has undergone numerous layers or chains of business rule processing and arrives at some End of Day, or End of Week or End of Month state. At this time it is collected, normalized, summarized and otherwise processed before being loaded in the DW.

An alternative approach is to siphon the data from the operational system flow as close to the transaction origination as possible. This data can then be made available for decision support. Granted, it may not have all of the checks and balances necessary for an accounting system but the timeliness of this raw, detailed data can have huge business benefit.

One reason for this value is that you are able to use the data to drive a strategy (and thus an action). If your users are not seeing the data as the operational systems see it, then you are creating strategy for situations that you will never be able to respond to as they happen.

This approach does not preclude the eventual updating or correcting of this data or providing a "more accurate" set of EOD, EOW or EOM data. In fact, both approaches can be complementary, and are necessary for different aspects of the business. If you load data as soon as it is created, you can always time box it. If you only load data based on a periodic reporting cycle, you can never "un-box it" and see the real business.

Windows of opportunity in today's business climate are measured in minutes, hours and days. Time is money. Waiting days or weeks for data can result in huge opportunity losses. Trimming the load process by 50% when that process is only 5% of the time from event origination to end user availability is focusing on the wrong problem.

Avoiding the Tar Pits

- *Understand the business value associated with data freshness.*
- *Establish data freshness Service Level Agreements.*
- *When seeking to improve data latency issues, consider the whole process, not just the final load.*
- *Look for opportunities to extract data from operational systems as close to the original event as possible.*
- *Use near real time data streaming or trickle-feed updating to make data available more quickly. Use Views to provide time-consistent data to the end users.*

Mistaking Time to Respond with Response Time

Tardy Measures are most dangerous when the occasion requires prompt action.
- Machiavelli

In the previous "entanglement" we addressed the confusion around the timeliness of data. There is a similar situation that occurs with query performance and providing timely answers to business questions. How many times have we encountered a scenario such as the following. IT Professional: "Here is the answer to the business question you asked. And look, it runs in less than 5 seconds. Isn't that awesome?" Business Professional: "But I needed the answer last week!"

To be fair, there are many applications where the same query will be executed hundreds of thousands of times. In these cases the database is an extension of the application. The requirements are well defined and stable. There will be hundreds of users executing exactly the same query while modifying only the search values (parameters). These types of queries are the mainstay of operational environments. These queries and their associated data structures (probably highly denormalized) will typically be tuned for the best possible response time. In this case the months of design, code, test and tuning are justified.

But sometimes we in IT spend more time in micro-optimization than is appropriate to the task at hand. We become too focused on the system issues and lose sight of the overall picture. We heard of a data warehousing shop in Europe where they were proud of the fact that queries were not running longer than five seconds. They viewed this as evidence of a successful data warehouse. What we learned is that queries running longer than 5 seconds were disallowed and cancelled.

There are other classes of business questions that are potentially far more important to the business. With these business questions, the most critical measure of responsiveness begins when the business user expresses a need for an answer or a limited set of business information and ends when the information is provided to him/her. In a large number of cases the value of the information diminishes significantly within hours of the original request.

The business value of these queries can be orders of magnitude greater than the typical predefined, canned and tuned queries. Why? Predefined queries tend to automate known business processes and deliver expected responses. But this second class of query usually delivers insight that was not anticipated. This class of query often leads to follow up, unanticipated queries where the answer is again needed in a matter of hours or less.

In this investigative environment of data warehousing and decision support, the business needs the ability to get answers to unanticipated business questions very quickly. They also need the ability to "fail fast." By "fail fast" we mean the need to submit a number of possibly important business questions where the potential value will not be fully understood until the answer is returned. In many cases the answers to these queries will be discarded but they may lead to additional queries where the answers have a significant impact. To "fail fast," there should be an absolute minimum of tuning and preparation for the query. This will lower the "pain threshold" of the "fast failure." If it only takes a few minutes to see if further analysis is necessary then more users will ask more investigative questions.

Avoiding the Tar Pits

- *Measure responsiveness based on delivering the answer to a business question rather than on system query performance. (This will encompass the people processes that surround the system activity.)*
- *Create a DSS environment that encourages "what if" and investigative business questions.*
- *Distinguish between canned queries that will be executed hundreds or thousands of times by numerous users from those that will be executed a few times by one or two users.*
- *Remember that a collection of these ad hoc business questions may prove to be more valuable to the business in the long run than the canned queries that implement known processes and usually yield predictable results.*
- *Implement different, very light weight, streamlined "processes" for handling these ad hoc or investigative business questions.*
- *Never place a short, artificial constraint on query run time.*
- *If you are creating reports, start looking at what actions are being taken off those reports. If there are none, get rid of the report. If there are some, can they be automated?*

The essence of being human is that one does not seek perfection.
– George Orwell

In this book we are concerned with excellence in data warehousing. But the pursuit of excellence carried to an extreme becomes perfectionism and perfectionism can destroy a data warehouse project.

Data warehousing is about learning and evolving while delivering business value along the way. It is a journey, not a destination. Perfectionism wants to arrive at the supposed ideal destination without the journey.

A good plan well executed is better than a perfect plan that never gets started.

How does perfectionism manifest itself in data warehousing?

- Attempting to define a complete and unchanging enterprise data model before moving to the next phase of system design. We have seen enterprise data model efforts that last for years while the business and the implementers wait for the perfect model.
- "Religious fervor" surrounding a certain "ideal" data warehouse architecture and data design approach that precludes the use of effective alternative approaches.
- Investing an inordinate amount of time and resources designing an answer to a business question when a simple, "raw" answer delivered in a timely manner would have been more valuable.

A phone directory company was implementing a data warehouse. The data model designed during the first phase was driven primarily by the data structure in the source systems. In some areas it was a fairly normalized design but other areas needed work and would not provide a good foundation over the long term. The data modeling team had identified these issues and were mandating that the changes be made to the model. But to implement all of the changes at once would have added 6 months to the time required to develop the extract, transformation and load processes. Rather than prioritizing the changes and implementing them in phases, the data modeling group attempted to force their "ideal" design. They were overruled and because they were unwilling to consider a phased implementation of the changes, none of the changes were implemented. How much better it would have been to accept a "good" solution, begin delivering business value, and implement the improvements over time.

Avoiding the Tar Pits

- *Be certain that you retain your focus on business priorities and delivering business value. Sometimes we in IT can become so enamored with a supposed ideal technical solution that we lose sight of business priorities.*
- *Implement firm time boxes around each phase of the project. Don't let the endless pursuit of a "better" design prevent you from delivering a good design on time.*

- *It is good to constantly strive to make the system better but you must deliver value in the mean time.*
- *Design and implement in relatively short phases and fund the data warehousing project as an ongoing infrastructure effort. People will sometimes attempt to force too much into a release or phase because they fear the subsequent phase or release will be too far out or will not be funded.*
- *Learn to "fail fast." Again, data warehousing is about learning and sometimes a better design or approach does not become evident until you begin implementing and using. Experience is a great teacher.*

The future belongs to those who see possibilities before they become obvious.
- John Sculley.

To quote John Foster Dulles, "The measure of success is not whether you have a tough problem to deal with, but whether it is the same problem you had last year." You have heard us say many times that data warehousing is a journey, not a destination. Excellence is a pursuit, not an achievement. Perfection does not exist. There are always new opportunities to serve the business and change the business through improved data warehousing and decision support.

Evolving your data warehouse to achieve excellence and continually realize business value requires leadership and vision. At a large financial institution, the data warehousing and decision support visionary on the business side left the company 18 months after phase one of the data warehouse was complete. Without that vision, the data warehouse stopped evolving and became consumed in the morass of "adequate", uninteresting IT systems where the business value had long since stopped increasing.

We know that there are many who are cynical about "vision" and mission statements and long term strategies. They live in an urgent world of here and now. Their heartburn stems from issues like data quality, why a query returned zero rows or why the loads did not run last night. In their mind and in their daily experience, vision is nice but irrelevant.

Those managers, architects and designers who are not involved in those critical low level issues and challenges have their own reasons for rolling their eyes at "vision." To them, vision means 2-3 years away. They are concerned with what the business needs this week, this month or this quarter.

These people are right! Vision is not about solving today's problems or deliver today's solutions. It is about doing today's work in a manner that will make it easier, more cost effective and, in some cases, possible to solve tomorrow's problems. Without vision the data warehouse devolves into a limited, reactive tool at best. More likely it will become stagnant and in the worst case it will lose funding and be jettisoned. Without an evolving vision the data warehouse effort will lose its way and die.

But vision must be translated into specific plans, deliverables and actions or it serves no purpose. A phrase made popular in the 1990's was "Think globally, act locally." In our case we could use a similar sentiment. Think in terms of two years, but act quarterly. You must deliver new business value each quarter, but that new capability must move you towards your two year goal.

This continuous delivery of new business value is the engine that keeps the data warehouse funded and growing. But an evolving vision will enable you to plan and blend important infrastructure and data enhancements into the quarterly releases. These in turn will yield a far more powerful, robust and cost effective environment in the future.

None of today's industry leading data warehouses began that way. They have grown and evolved. The business value they deliver today is orders of magnitude beyond where they began. New applications of data warehousing are implemented in a fraction of the cost and time that was the case in the past. They had a vision and they persisted in implementing that vision. If you want to achieve excellence in data warehousing, emulate them.

Avoiding the Tar Pits

- *What is the strategic vision for your data warehouse efforts? Where are you headed? If you don't have one now is the time.*
- *Review and refine your data warehouse vision at least once per year. Do this with full representation from corporate leadership, business leadership and IT.*
- *Don't allow the data warehouse vision to belong solely to one person. If that person leaves you lose your vision. The data warehouse is a corporate asset and should be driven by a corporate vision.*
- *Consider what other companies are doing. You can learn much from companies not only within your industry but also those outside your industry. User groups are a great opportunity to hear about the successes and learnings of other companies.*
- *Enable, Encourage, Embrace and evolve your strategic data warehouse vision. Make the vision real.*

Final commentary

Consensus is the absence of leadership
- Margaret Thatcher.

The bottom line of building and leveraging the data warehouse is to support action by giving business insight and improvement. This cannot be simply an exercise in technology. As Kevin Strange, of Gartner Group once wrote, "Data warehouses do not fail by accident. They do not succeed by accident either." In order to succeed, one must carefully plan and relentlessly execute those plans.

But what is behind the success, beyond hard work and determination? It can be seen by following the path, starting with the overriding thought that data warehousing is about the business.

Business is about focus. There is a saying that if you try to chase two rabbits, both will escape. In order to succeed, one must have clear focus on what you are trying to achieve. With focus, the data warehouse team can be directed and motivated to success.

Focus is about commitment. To have commitment you must have courage of your convictions. Undertaking the data warehouse is more often a political and cultural challenge than anything else. Unless you are committed to the cause and believe in it strongly enough to endure the critics and nay sayers, you cannot succeed.

Commitment is about leadership. It has been said that conviction is believing you are right; leadership is getting others to believe that as well. Leaders cannot hide since no one will follow. A leader must be out in front of the charge and showing the way by example. Barriers will be erected by others and you must be able and willing to knock those barriers down. When you show that you are personally dedicated to the success of the project, then others will gladly follow you through the rough spots.

Leadership is about vision. It is impossible to have all the preceding ingredients without a vision as to what you are trying to achieve. Where are you taking the business? What change are you bringing to the culture that will transform the company from a player to a leader? This vision will give you the focus, commitment and leadership to create a successful atmosphere. Failure is only an option when you are prepared to fail.

The book has given many examples of the types of success than can be achieved as well as a sampling of failures to avoid. Exploiting the warehouse means that you are never satisfied with the last success but are always looking for the next advantage that can be gained. In such an atmosphere the conviction is contagious and the successful evolution is guaranteed.

17188082R00078

Made in the USA
Lexington, KY
30 August 2012